S0-BNI-801

Chests and Cabinets

Editors of *Fine Woodworking*

The Taunton Press

Text © 2014 by The Taunton Press, Inc.
Photographs © 2014 by The Taunton Press, Inc.
Illustrations © 2014 by The Taunton Press, Inc.
All rights reserved.

THE TAUNTON PRESS, INC.
63 South Main Street, PO Box 5506
Newtown, CT 06470-5506
e-mail: tp@taunton.com

EDITOR: Christina Glennon
COPY EDITOR: Candace B. Levy
INDEXER: Jay Kreider
COVER & INTERIOR DESIGN: carol singer | notice design
LAYOUT: Cathy Cassidy

Fine Woodworking® is a trademark of The Taunton Press, Inc.,
registered in the U.S. Patent and Trademark Office

The following names/manufacturers appearing in *Fine Woodworking Chests and Cabinets* are trademarks: Accuride®, ApplePly®, Deft®, Festool®, Domino®, Forstner®, Freud®, Lee Valley Tools®, Melamine®, Minwax®, Tried &True™, Waterlox®, Zinnser® Bulls Eye®, Zinnser® Bulls Eye® SealCoat™.

LIBRARY OF CONGRESS CATALOGING-IN-PUBLICATION DATA

Fine woodworking chests and cabinets / editors of Fine woodworking.
    pages cm
  Includes index.
  ISBN 978-1-62710-712-9
  1. Chests. 2. Cabinetwork. I. Fine woodworking. II. Title: Chests and cabinets.
  TT197.F527 2014
  684.1'6--dc23
                    2014017190

PRINTED IN THE UNITED STATES OF AMERICA
10 9 8 7 6 5 4 3 2 1

This book is complied from articles that originally appeared in *Fine Woodworking* magazine. Unless otherwise noted, costs listed were current at the time the articles first appeared.

ABOUT YOUR SAFETY: Working wood is inherently dangerous. Using hand or power tools improperly or ignoring safety practices can lead to permanent injury or even death. Don't try to perform operations you learn about here (or elsewhere) unless you're certain they are safe for you. If something about an operation doesn't feel right, don't do it. Look for another way. We want you to enjoy the craft, so please keep safety foremost in your mind whenever you're in the shop.

ACKNOWLEDGMENTS

Special thanks to the authors, editors, art directors, copy editors, and other staff members of *Fine Woodworking* who contributed to the development of the chapters in this book.

Contents

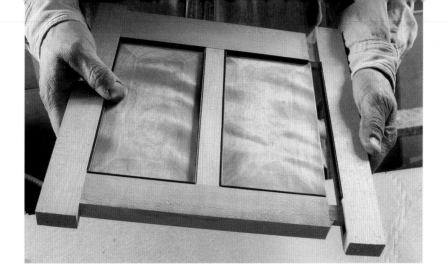

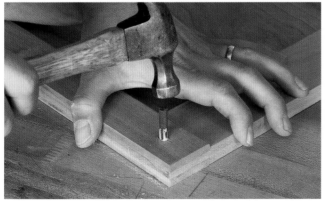

Introduction

One of the best things about *Fine Woodworking* magazine is the array of furniture projects we offer. From simple mitered boxes to tables to chests, we've done them all.

The hard part as a reader is waiting for that perfect project to appear in one of our six regular issues. That's because we can fit only two or three projects in an issue, and we have to offer a variety of pieces. So over the course of a year we may do only one chest of drawers, or one blanket chest. But with *Chests and Cabinets*, you get a collection of some of the best storage projects *Fine Woodworking* has published.

Our editors scoured the pages of the magazine, looking for a perfect mix of projects to meet all skill levels, and putting them all in one place. With this complete collection, you'll get detailed instructions and plans, paired with rich, informative photographs, to guide you through each project.

Best of all, you can get right to building. No need to worry or fret over design, or making prototypes to get a feel for scale and appearance. Our expert builders and designers have done it all for you, providing tasteful takes on all types of chests and cabinets, from period-perfect pieces to one-of-a-kind, modern designs.

You'll get classic Shaker designs for a blanket chest, a chest of drawers, and two types of cupboards for your dishware. You can build an Arts and Crafts display cabinet or bookcase, or take on the challenge of a vintage lowboy or Pennsylvania spicebox. You'll even get great designs for wall cabinets and bookcases. And each project is loaded with tips and tricks for getting the most out of both machine and hand tools, techniques you'll use down the road as you build more and more furniture.

I hope you have fun in the shop with these projects. Now it's time to get to work.

—Tom McKenna
Editor, *Fine Woodworking*

Shaker Blanket Chest

CHARLES DURFEE

The earliest storage chests were simple boxes made of six boards. As they evolved, a base, or plinth, was added to lift them off the floor and give them aesthetic appeal. Although molding the edges created a more finished look, anyone who used such a chest soon found that they had to fish around for small items that ended up on the bottom. To solve this problem, furniture makers added first one drawer, and then two or even three drawers. Finally, the lid was eliminated, leaving a full chest of drawers as we know it today.

During the evolution from blanket box to chest of drawers, the grain in the sides changed from horizontal to vertical. Many of the single-drawer versions exhibit an intermediate stage in this evolution, with vertical grain in the sides nailed to horizontal grain in the front, which probably is the only way they could be joined. In this piece, the older style with all horizontal grain is retained, which enables the front, back, and sides to be joined with dovetails. As long as the sides don't get too tall, this is a superior form of construction: Seasonal wood movement results in the parts moving together, instead of against each other.

Match the dimensions to your hand-picked boards

Although the Shakers probably would have used painted pine, modern woodworkers may prefer the natural look of fine wood. I used some excellent single-log Pennsylvania cherry with lots of curl, nicely matched in grain and color.

You may need to adjust the overall dimensions if you want to use specific boards in particular places. In this case, I made the overall height a bit less than planned so that I could use an exceptionally fine single-width board for the front. You can lay out the actual dimensions on a story stick, using one face each for height, width, and depth. The story stick will give you all of the information necessary to begin construction, so you won't need any drawings.

After double-checking to ensure planning and layout make sense, mill and glue the boards for the front, sides, back, top, and drawer front. Leave the inner bottom oversize; it should be sized to just fit into its grooves. In addition, you can make up the bottom frame-and-panel. Remove any dry excess glue and flatten the boards using planes or sanders and a straightedge. To save time, I take the parts to a local mill shop and run them through a thickness sander.

With the case front, back, and sides cut to size, run the grooves for the inner bottom (on the front, the groove technically is a rabbet).

(continued on p. 8)

Dovetailed Blanket Chest with a Drawer

Because of the drawer, the front corners have fewer dovetails than the rear corners. The dovetail spacing may be slightly different on the back than on the front but should appear to be the same.

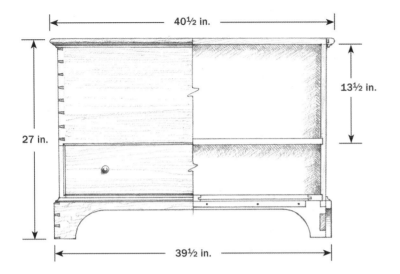

40½ in.

13½ in.

27 in.

39½ in.

19¾ in.

21¼ in.

5 in.

20 in.

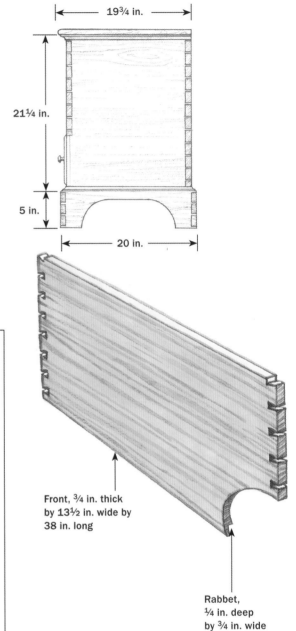

Front, ¾ in. thick by 13½ in. wide by 38 in. long

Rabbet, ¼ in. deep by ¾ in. wide

LIPPED-FRONT DRAWER

The cherry drawer front is lipped on the top and sides. The sides, back, and bottom of the drawer are made of a secondary wood.

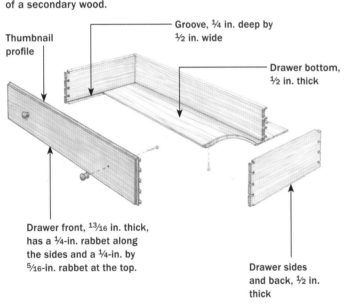

Thumbnail profile

Groove, ¼ in. deep by ½ in. wide

Drawer bottom, ½ in. thick

Drawer front, ¹³⁄₁₆ in. thick, has a ¼-in. rabbet along the sides and a ¼-in. by ⁵⁄₁₆-in. rabbet at the top.

Drawer sides and back, ½ in. thick

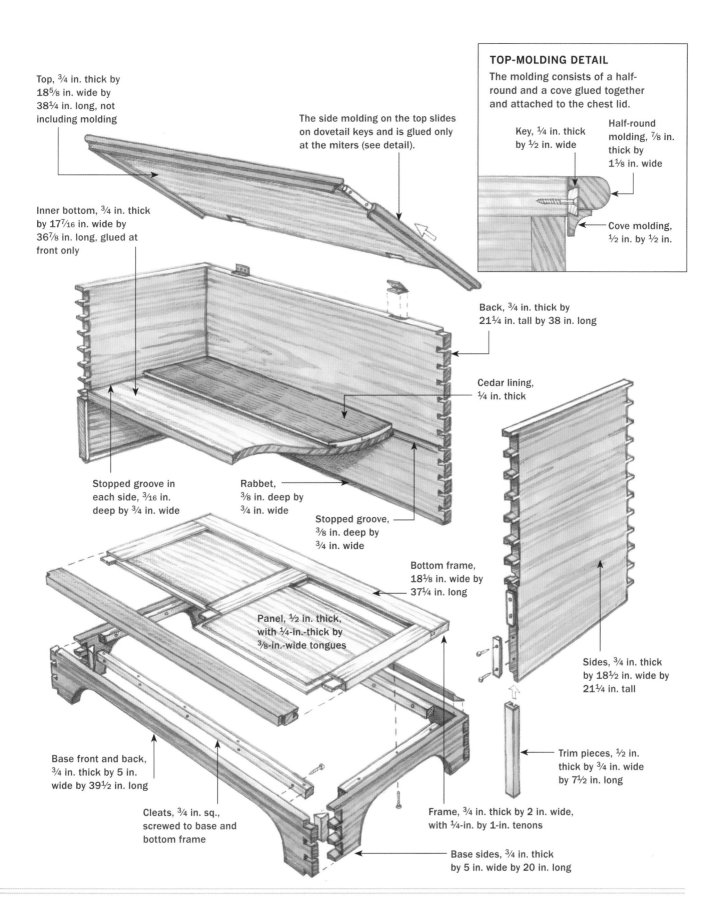

Top, ¾ in. thick by 18⅝ in. wide by 38¼ in. long, not including molding

The side molding on the top slides on dovetail keys and is glued only at the miters (see detail).

(see detail)

TOP-MOLDING DETAIL
The molding consists of a half-round and a cove glued together and attached to the chest lid.

Key, ¼ in. thick by ½ in. wide

Half-round molding, ⅞ in. thick by 1⅛ in. wide

Cove molding, ½ in. by ½ in.

Inner bottom, ¾ in. thick by 17⁷⁄₁₆ in. wide by 36⅞ in. long, glued at front only

Back, ¾ in. thick by 21¼ in. tall by 38 in. long

Cedar lining, ¼ in. thick

Stopped groove in each side, ³⁄₁₆ in. deep by ¾ in. wide

Rabbet, ⅜ in. deep by ¾ in. wide

Stopped groove, ⅜ in. deep by ¾ in. wide

Bottom frame, 18⅛ in. wide by 37¼ in. long

Panel, ½ in. thick, with ¼-in.-thick by ⅜-in.-wide tongues

Sides, ¾ in. thick by 18½ in. wide by 21¼ in. tall

Base front and back, ¾ in. thick by 5 in. wide by 39½ in. long

Cleats, ¾ in. sq., screwed to base and bottom frame

Frame, ¾ in. thick by 2 in. wide, with ¼-in. by 1-in. tenons

Trim pieces, ½ in. thick by ¾ in. wide by 7½ in. long

Base sides, ¾ in. thick by 5 in. wide by 20 in. long

Lay out the dovetails. Use a pair of dividers to lay out the dovetails evenly. The spacing on the front corners may need to be slightly different from the spacing on the rear due to the presence of the drawer.

Extend the layout to the end of the board. After marking the tails on the face of the board with a sliding bevel, extend the lines across the end of the board using a square and a knife. The knife cuts will help guide the saw as you cut.

Line up the boards. Before laying out the pins, ensure that the boards are flat and meet at 90°.

Mark the pins from the tails. With the boards secure, use a sharp pencil to transfer the location of the pins. A flashlight helps you see into the corners.

The grooves need to be stopped before the ends and carefully aligned from the top so that all four grooves match up. I use a ¾-in. straight bit in a plunge router and run the tool against a straightedge to ensure a straight cut. Make the rabbet for the frame-and-panel bottom in the same fashion, stopped at the rear corners only.

Construct the carcase with dovetails

There are a lot of dovetails to cut in this project, so you might as well decide on a method of cutting them and stick with it. If you use a router setup, make sure the jig can handle the long row of the rear corners or has a way to index setups. I cut the dovetails with hand tools, which mostly is an exercise in marking and sawing accurately.

When laying out the joints, aim for a spacing between pins of about 1¾ in. on-center. This chest has the peculiar problem of the front and back rows being different lengths, due to the drawer opening. Try to have the front series end with a small half pin or a small half tail, for appearance's sake. Make your scribe marks on the front edge of the sides down to the drawer opening only.

When cutting the dovetails, orient the outside face of the side toward you. Begin sawcuts at the top back corner; come across the top edge to set the saw in and then down the front face at an angle, keeping the saw completely in the kerf. Then finish the cut by raising the handle gradually. To ensure the cut is made to its full depth, I follow an old-timer's practice of cutting slightly past the scribe on the back side. After cutting the tails, check that they are square and do any necessary paring. In this way, any adjustments to get a good fit are done on only the pins.

Use the tails to mark the pins

When marking from one part to the next, make sure the front and back are perfectly square to each side and that the grooves line up so that the inner bottom will be able to slide in. I use a very sharp pencil lead extended from a lead holder for marking. It leaves a fine line, is much easier to see than a knife scribe, and doesn't accidentally cut the tail.

With the case dovetailing done, cut the recesses for the trim pieces on the lower front edges of the sides.

Assemble the chest in stages. Gluing this many dovetails is stressful enough without trying to do all of them at once. Before you start, make some cauls on the bandsaw to fit over the protruding pins. (1) First glue the front to the two sides and slide in the inner bottom, gluing the front edge into the rabbet and allowing the rest to float. (2) When this first assembly has dried, glue on the back, again using the cauls. (3) When the back is dry, fit and glue the frame-and-panel base into the bottom rabbet.

When Things Go Wrong With Your Dovetails

Hand-cut dovetails should not be perfect and indeed rarely will be. However, some faults that occur during fitting or assembly need to be repaired because they detract from the overall appearance of the piece.

WHEN A TEST FIT CRACKS THE WOOD

When dry-fitting dovetails, it takes only one too-tight pin to cause a crack. This needs to be repaired before the two boards are dovetailed together. It's difficult to force glue down into the crack, but by placing the board half hanging off the bench and then flexing it while pushing the glue into the crack with your finger, you can work the glue in from both sides until the joint is saturated. Place waxed paper over the joint to protect the clamp that keeps the two sides of the crack parallel, and then place another clamp across the board to pull the crack together.

Repair a crack. While flexing the board up and down, force glue into the crack (left). Use one clamp to keep both sides of the crack aligned, with waxed paper between the glue and clamp; then close the crack with another clamp across the board (below).

UNSIGHTLY GAPS BETWEEN PINS AND TAILS

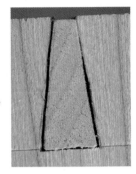

Don't despair if there are gaps on either side of the pins and tails. If the gaps are very narrow, you can repair them by inserting some glue and peening the tail or pin with a ball-peen hammer. The blows spread out the end grain until it fills the gaps. This method requires that the tail or pin protrude at least 1/16 in. because it will be necessary to plane away the crushed surface end grain.

If the gaps are wide, the best way to fill them is by tapping in a thin wedge lubricated with a little glue. After the glue has dried, saw off the protruding part of the wedge and smooth the surface with a block plane. The end grain of the wedge will be an almost perfect match with the pin or tail.

Peen small gaps. Small gaps can be filled by inserting a little glue and then hitting the pin or tail with a ball-peen hammer. Do this before planing the pins flush so that the hammer marks can be removed.

Shim larger gaps. A narrow wedge driven into the gap beside a pin will make an almost invisible end-grain repair.

Dry-fit the carcase before final assembly

When dry-fitting the case parts, push the joints together as much as possible by hand, then use a rubber mallet. When the joints are almost there, resort to clamps. You walk a fine line when fitting exposed dovetails: Too tight, and you risk splitting the wood; too loose, and you leave gaps between the pins and tails. Fortunately, splits and gaps can be fixed (see "When Things Go Wrong with Your Dovetails" on the facing page).

For the glue-up, I make special clamp cauls (see the photos on p. 9) to span the pins because they protrude somewhat. To make the glue-up less nerve-wracking, break down the process into steps. Assemble the front, the two sides, and the inner bottom as a unit first. The front edge of the inner bottom is glued only to the front rabbet (the rest is left unglued to allow for seasonal movement). If necessary, cut a temporary spacer to hold the rear edges in the correct alignment. The second step is to glue on the back. When the back is dry, fit and glue the base frame into the bottom rabbet.

Trim Pieces Hide the End Grain

Trim pieces are attached with sliding dovetail keys that allow for seasonal movement. The pieces stop short of the bottom by ¼ in., with the gap concealed by the cove molding of the base.

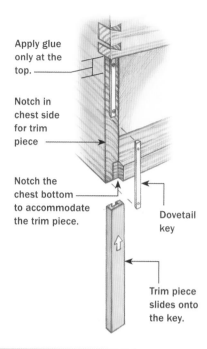

Apply glue only at the top.

Notch in chest side for trim piece

Notch the chest bottom to accommodate the trim piece.

Dovetail key

Trim piece slides onto the key.

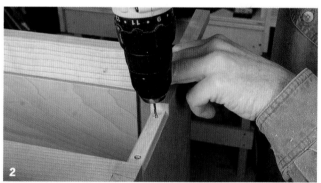

Cap the end grain. To conceal the end grain, the sides are notched adjacent to the drawer, and trim pieces are attached over dovetail keys. (1) After assembling the case, notch the case bottom where it intersects the sides. (2) Then screw the dovetail key to the case using the trim piece to aid alignment. (3) Finally, saw apart the key to allow for seasonal movement of the case. Glue the trim piece only at the top.

Install the Bracket Base

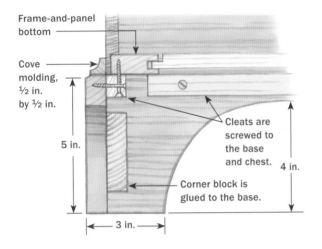

Frame-and-panel bottom

Cove molding, ½ in. by ½ in.

5 in.

Cleats are screwed to the base and chest.

Corner block is glued to the base.

4 in.

3 in.

1

Save the waste piece. After cutting the profile of the base, save the offcuts, which can be cut in two and used as clamping cauls when gluing together the base.

2

Attach the cleats. Screw cleats to all four sides of the base. Then drive screws up through each cleat to attach the base to the chest.

Conceal the end grain with trim pieces

With the carcase assembled, cut a notch in the base frame at each front corner for the trim pieces. On original Shaker chests, these trim pieces as well as the moldings were simply nailed on, which not only caused seasonal wood-movement problems but also were aesthetically unpleasing in an unpainted piece. A more elegant solution is to attach these cross-grain parts with sliding dovetail keys. I vary this method slightly, screwing the key on beginning at the inboard end and pulling off the molding, fastening as I go. The segments are cut out and the molding slid back on with glue at the inboard end. Leave the bottom end of the trim pieces about ¼ in. short of the case bottom to allow for seasonal expansion. The cove molding will cover the gap.

3

Fit the molding. Because the grain on the chest runs horizontally, the base molding can be glued to both the base and the sides.

Build the base and the top before attaching the molding

On this chest, the base runs around all four sides, as opposed to most Early American chests, which have bracket bases on the front and sides only. Saw the dovetails first and then cut out the profile on the bandsaw; you can save the cutouts to use as clamp cauls. Nail a plywood template to the back of the base pieces and clean up the profile on the router table with a top-guided bearing bit. Screw cleats to the inside of the base and drive screws through the cleats to attach the base to the chest.

Because the moldings overlap the top edge of the case, the top should be sized so that the front clearance is proportional to the amount of seasonal wood movement. I built this chest in the winter, and the wood's moisture content was 6%, so I sized the top with a minimal clearance of a strong $\frac{1}{16}$ in. ($\frac{3}{16}$ in. to $\frac{1}{4}$ in. should be sufficient clearance for a summer-built chest).

The top molding consists of a half-round and a cove made on the router table and then glued together. While you're at it, make some extra cove molding for the base. The front piece is mitered and glued to the top, while the sides are installed over dovetail keys, with glue at the miters only.

The drawer front is in the traditional style, lipped on the top and sides and molded all around. The sides and back on my drawer are quartersawn pine, and the bottom is poplar. You can find quartered stock at any lumberyard—just look through a stack of boards for ones with growth rings perpendicular to the board's face.

Cut the drawer front first, with its side rabbets trimmed so that they just fit into the opening. The top rabbet needs to have only about $\frac{1}{16}$ in. of clearance because seasonal movement of the drawer will be in the same direction as the case. Cut the dovetails by hand, but use a Forstner® bit to drill out the bulk of the waste between the half-blind pins.

Attach the hardware and finish the piece

By now you will have something that looks like a chest. The top is secured with mortised-in butt hinges. I used extruded-brass hinges from Whitechapel (www.whitechapel-ltd. com), but you may opt for a more authentic style with thinner leaves. When the top is fastened, find the location for the stay. I used a brass chain, which isn't strictly traditional Shaker but still shares a similar simplicity.

Throughout the construction process, you should have been planing, scraping, and/or sanding to all but the final passes. I generally take out machine marks (including the tracks left by the thickness sander) with a handplane and scraper. The final work is done with a 220-grit disk in a random-orbit sander.

I used Minwax® Antique Oil Finish, but any oil/varnish mixture will work well. The first coat is always exciting—the figure fairly jumps off the surface—but it also reveals any dents, dings, and glue splotches that should be wet sanded with finish using 220-grit or higher sandpaper.

After the finishing is completed, add the thin cedar lining in the chest bottom. I used some leftover western red cedar clapboards. I planed them down, shiplapped the edges, and tacked them in, leaving them unfinished. Years hence, a light sanding will refresh the smell, allowing me to recall the pleasure of building this piece.

Hickory and Ash Blanket Chest

PETER TURNER

When thumbing through furniture books, I find myself drawn to long, low chests, similar to the wooden chests my folks had in our living room when I was a kid. So when I was invited to participate as a guest artist in the New Hampshire Furniture Masters Association's 2008 auction, a blanket chest was one of the three proposals I submitted, and this is the piece the jury chose.

To present my proposal, I offered scaled drawings that gave top, front, and end views. The process of drawing usually lets my mind walk through the fabrication so I'm sure the piece will work. Everything comes off the drawings. When things get tricky, like

Legs Are the Cornerstones

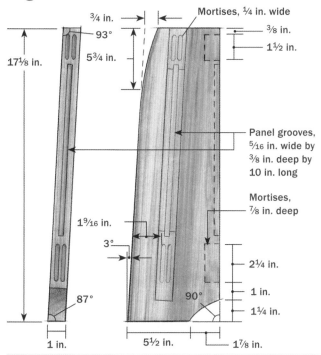

Mortises, ¼ in. wide

¾ in.

93°

17⅛ in.

5¾ in.

⅜ in.

1½ in.

Panel grooves,
⁵⁄₁₆ in. wide by
⅜ in. deep by
10 in. long

Mortises,
⅞ in. deep

1⁹⁄₁₆ in.

3°

2¼ in.

1 in.

1¼ in.

87°

90°

1 in.

5½ in.

1⅞ in.

A simple jig establishes the angle. To keep the grain parallel with the outside slant of the leg, the author tapers the inside edge.

Now cut the legs to length. Putting the inside edge against the fence means you can avoid cutting a compound angle on the ends. A simple 3° blade tilt does the job.

Taper the Legs First

Plywood base

Clamp

3°

Fence

angled or intricate joinery, I go back to them, laying pieces right on the full-size drawings to physically check measurements and angles. I did full-sizers of the leg blank and the ends, and to be extra sure, I made story sticks to lay out the frames and panels.

The legs of this frame-and-panel chest serve as end pieces for the front, back, and end frames. The top and panels are ash; the frames are hickory. I applied battens to the one-piece top to keep it flat. I kept all thicknesses beefy for heft and used double floating tenons for strength. To emphasize the length of the chest, the grain of the panels runs horizontally.

To keep the construction manageable, all the angles are the same, off from square by 3°. First, the angle is found on the outside top and bottom of each leg. Next, the end frames and panels also get the 3° angle, but the front and back frames and panels don't, which means the end joinery is angled but the front and rear are not. The front and rear

assemblies lean into the angle on the end assemblies, so the tops of all the long top rails will need the angle too.

I favor floating tenons because of their efficiency when dealing with angled joinery. They are as strong as any integral tenon, and you don't need to fit angled shoulders—you just make simple butt joints. After planing my tenon stock to fit a test mortise, I rounded both edges of the stock on the router table and scored both faces with two shallow kerfs for glue relief. With a few crosscuts, I had my tenons.

Blanket Chest

A straightforward approach to angled joinery simplifies the construction of this frame-and-panel chest, while thick parts and dense woods (ash and hickory) lend heft to a sleek design.

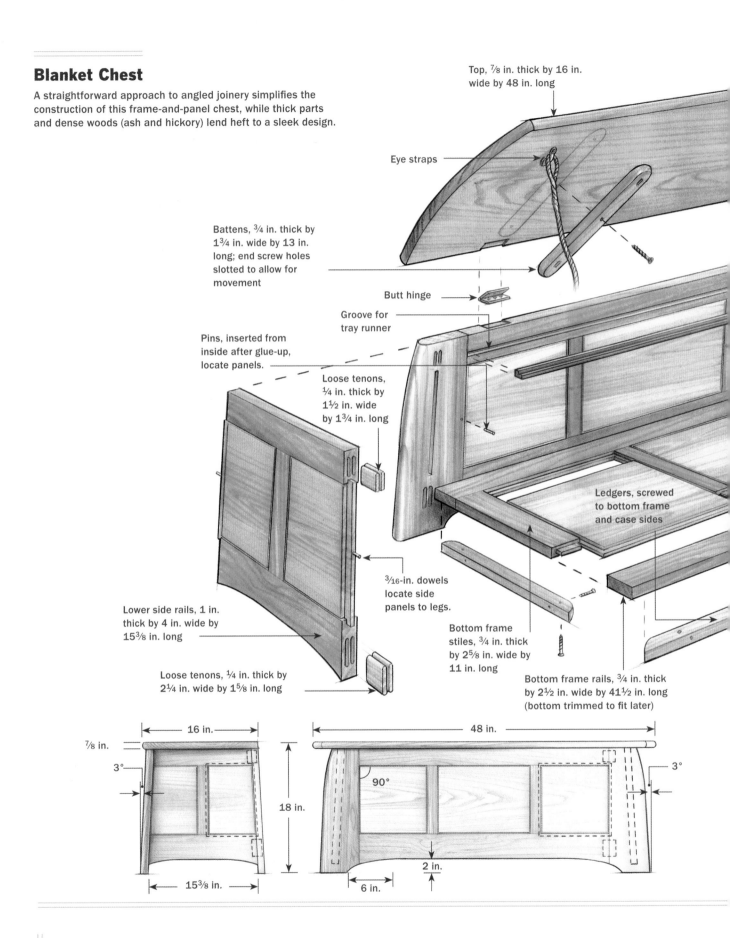

Top, ⅞ in. thick by 16 in. wide by 48 in. long

Eye straps

Battens, ¾ in. thick by 1¾ in. wide by 13 in. long; end screw holes slotted to allow for movement

Butt hinge

Groove for tray runner

Pins, inserted from inside after glue-up, locate panels.

Loose tenons, ¼ in. thick by 1½ in. wide by 1¾ in. long

Ledgers, screwed to bottom frame and case sides

Lower side rails, 1 in. thick by 4 in. wide by 15⅜ in. long

³⁄₁₆-in. dowels locate side panels to legs.

Bottom frame stiles, ¾ in. thick by 2⅝ in. wide by 11 in. long

Loose tenons, ¼ in. thick by 2¼ in. wide by 1⅝ in. long

Bottom frame rails, ¾ in. thick by 2½ in. wide by 41½ in. long (bottom trimmed to fit later)

16 in.

⅞ in.

3°

18 in.

15⅜ in.

48 in.

90°

3°

2 in.

6 in.

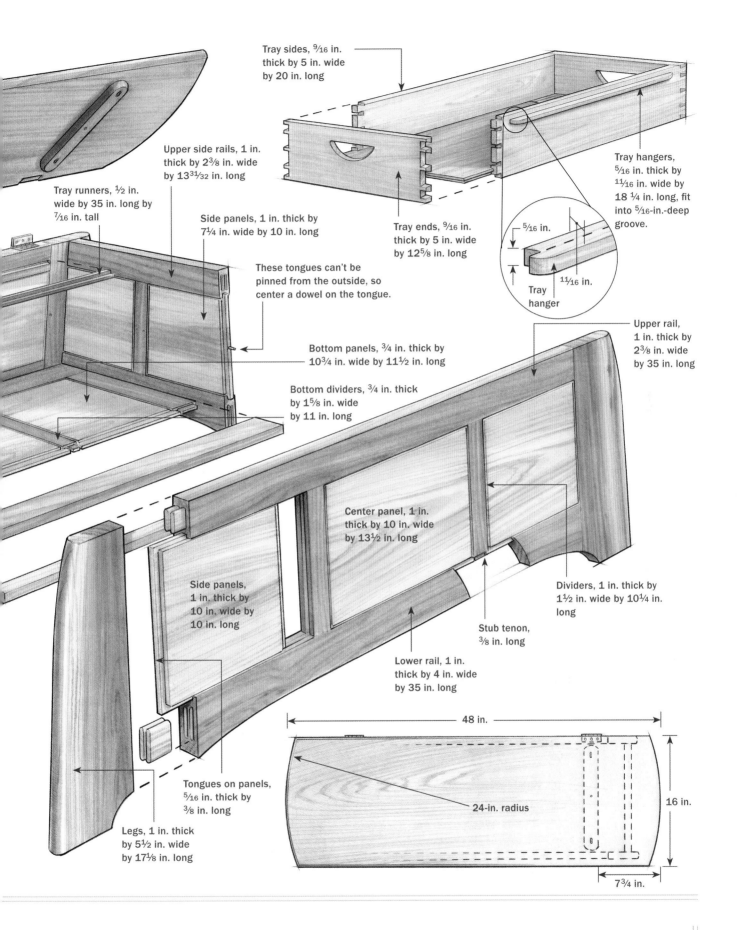

Tray sides, 9/16 in. thick by 5 in. wide by 20 in. long

Upper side rails, 1 in. thick by 2 3/8 in. wide by 13 31/32 in. long

Tray runners, 1/2 in. wide by 35 in. long by 7/16 in. tall

Side panels, 1 in. thick by 7 1/4 in. wide by 10 in. long

These tongues can't be pinned from the outside, so center a dowel on the tongue.

Tray ends, 9/16 in. thick by 5 in. wide by 12 5/8 in. long

Tray hangers, 5/16 in. thick by 11/16 in. wide by 18 1/4 in. long, fit into 5/16-in.-deep groove.

5/16 in.

11/16 in.

Tray hanger

Bottom panels, 3/4 in. thick by 10 3/4 in. wide by 11 1/2 in. long

Bottom dividers, 3/4 in. thick by 1 5/8 in. wide by 11 in. long

Upper rail, 1 in. thick by 2 3/8 in. wide by 35 in. long

Center panel, 1 in. thick by 10 in. wide by 13 1/2 in. long

Side panels, 1 in. thick by 10 in. wide by 10 in. long

Dividers, 1 in. thick by 1 1/2 in. wide by 10 1/4 in. long

Stub tenon, 3/8 in. long

Lower rail, 1 in. thick by 4 in. wide by 35 in. long

Tongues on panels, 5/16 in. thick by 3/8 in. long

Legs, 1 in. thick by 5 1/2 in. wide by 17 1/8 in. long

48 in.

24-in. radius

16 in.

7 3/4 in.

Create compound-angled legs

Generally, I like to start with the trickiest joinery. That way, I can get the most difficult parts finished and know it will only get easier as I go. On this chest, the mortises on the legs and rail ends called loudest to go first. Before I cut any mortises, I had to create the angles in the legs. By removing the wedge from the inside of the leg rather than the outside, I kept the grain orientation parallel to the leg's outer slanting edge. Then I cut them to length at an angle, which establishes the only compound angles in the piece (see photos on p. 15).

Cut mortises in pairs

Nearly all the parts of this chest are 1 in. thick. The weight called for substantial joinery, so I doubled the tenons to create twice the glue surface. There are a lot of mortises to cut in the leg edges, leg faces, and all the rail ends. I used a basic spacer method on the edge guide of my router to give me repeatability so that all the pairs of double mortises would match.

Face mortises. Run the router's edge guide along the outside edge when cutting both face and edge mortises. After cutting the first set of mortises, the author attaches a spacer with double-faced tape (top) to bump out the edge guide and make the second set of mortises parallel to the first (above).

Same method for edge mortises. When cutting double mortises on the leg edges, stack two legs to give the router base more surface to ride on.

Mortise and shape the rails. End rails have angled shoulders. The author cuts the 3° angle on one end of the rail and then uses a full-size drawing to mark the length (left) of the other end. He uses a simple vise-mounted jig when mortising the ends. It holds the rails square and gives a surface for the edge guide to ride on. The jig works for the angled rails too (right).

To cut the leg face mortises, transfer the locations from the drawing and use a plunge router with an adjustable edge guide. Though the tenons come in at an angle, I cut the mortises perpendicular to the leg face. The time savings makes up for the bit of glue surface that must be trimmed from the tenons.

I mortised the leg edges by again using a plunge router with an edge guide. To give the router base more surface to ride on, I stacked two legs together, flush at the angled edge. For the rail ends, I used a jig that mounts in my bench vise. For all of these doubled mortises, use the same spacer for the second cut.

Later, I used a dado blade to cut grooves in the rails and dividers that hold the panels. But the panel grooves in the leg faces and leg edges cannot go through or they will be visible, so while you're working on the legs and the router is out, plunge-rout all of these stopped grooves with a 5/16-in. straight bit. Square up the ends by hand.

Cut the curve in the lower rails. Once the mortises are cut, the author bandsaws the curve of the lower rails close to the line and then template-routs the final curve.

Groove the Rails

All of the panel grooves are square, but the long top rails need an angled groove for the tray runner.

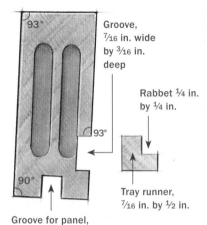

Groove, 7/16 in. wide by 3/16 in. deep

Rabbet 1/4 in. by 1/4 in.

Tray runner, 7/16 in. by 1/2 in.

Groove for panel, 5/16 in. wide by 3/8 in. deep

93°
93°
90°

Angle the dado set. Use a bevel gauge to ensure that the dado blade matches the 3° angle on the rest of the blanket chest.

Cut the groove. Once the dado blade is tilted, set the blade height and cut a through-groove to hold the tray runner.

Once all the mortises and grooves are cut, bandsaw the curves that define the feet and give the lower rails their final shape. After glue-up, you'll return to the spots where the feet meet the bottom rails and refine the curve.

Panels and dividers are tongue-and-groove

After the mortises, it's time to work on the dividers, rails, and panels. Using multiple passes over the tablesaw blade and a stop clamped to the crosscut sled, cut stub tenons on both ends of the dividers. Then, using a dado set, cut grooves for the panels in the edges of the dividers.

Without changing the dado-blade setting, run the straight grooves (for the panels and divider tenons) in the long rails. And while the dado set is still in the tablesaw, make the angled grooves for the tray runners in the inside faces of the long upper rails. Finally, rip the angle on the top edge of the upper rails.

I like the look of uninterrupted surfaces on the same plane, so rather than inserting thin panels in a groove, I used thick panels and

Bevel the top edges. After switching back to a rip blade, the top edge of the top rails must also be cut to the 3° angle.

cut a tongue in the center to keep the faces of the panels flush with the frame. First I cut the angle on the outside edges of the end panels. Then I cut the tongues on the tablesaw.

Cut tongues on the tablesaw. With the panels facedown, cut around the edges on all sides. Then ride the panel on edge and cut off the rest of the waste material, leaving the tongue. Keep the panel between the blade and the fence so the offcuts fall to the outside of the blade.

Make the panels. The side panels are tapered. To angle the outside edges, the author uses the same jig he used to cut the angle on the legs.

Glue up in stages: front and back first. The author uses Unibond 800 for more open time. Place the center panel into the bottom rail, add the dividers and then the end panels, set the top rail on, and add the legs last (left). Center marks help locate the dividers and keep everything evenly spaced. Angled cauls keep the clamps aligned. Next, the author uses a coping saw to cut the curve at the top of each leg and then uses a block plane to take it to its final shape (right).

Add the ends. Lay the front assembly face down and add the end rails. Slide in the first panel, then the divider, and then the second panel (far left). Once you add the back assembly, gently turn the whole thing upside down and clamp securely (left). Use the same angled clamping cauls as before.

Glue up in sections

Start the glue-up with the front and back, each with two legs, two long rails, two dividers, and three panels. Use angled cauls and pipe clamps to help distribute pressure.

Once the front and back assemblies have cured, pin the panels in place from the inside with toothpicks. This keeps the gaps even as the solid panels expand and contract. Pinning the panels after the glue-up works with the front and back frames but doesn't work on the ends of the chest, where the panels fit into the face of the leg. There, I used a dowel centered in the tongue and groove.

After finish-sanding the interior, it is time to add the short sides (two angled short rails, one divider, and two panels per side), reusing the angled cauls to clamp the case. Take care that all top rails sit flush with the legs, or you'll have to take great pains to flush everything up after the glue-up.

While this assembly is drying, glue and clamp the bottom frame (two rails, two dividers, and three panels), and set it aside to fit into the case later.

Hinge the lid after glue-up is complete

On a one-piece top, I like to orient the lid's end grain so that the rings look like smiles. Then, at some point in the future, if it wants to cup, the front edge of the lid should dive into the front of the chest rather than up and away.

Rout the rear rail for its hinges. Place the oversize lid on the chest to adjust its position. Once you're sure about the placement of the lid, use the mortises in the rail to mark and then rout the corresponding mortises in the lid. By mounting the lid, you can test its fit again, mark and cut its finished dimensions, and grab a measurement for the rope stop.

With the top cut to length, I used a template and router with a flush-trimming bit to cut the lid to shape. I made a full-size template for the end curves, but before using the template and the router to cut the shape, I wasted away close to the line with the bandsaw. From there I used a handheld router and a ½-in. roundover bit with bearing to shape the ends and front edge to their final profile, a roundover with a distinct sharp edge.

Sliding tray glides on shopmade runners

The carcase glue-up gives interior dimensions for both the dovetailed sliding tray and the frame-and-panel bottom.

Cut the rabbet for the chest-mounted tray runners from wide stock on the tablesaw. Then rip the pieces to width. Chop the runners to length to exactly match the length of the upper rails. Give both ends a curve and then glue them into the front and back rails of the chest. It's important that the runners be fully seated in their grooves so that they provide maximum support for the sliding hangers.

After hand-cutting the dovetails, rout stopped grooves on the outside top of the tray

Install the Bottom and Top

Bevel the bottom and test-fit, repeating until the fit is snug.

Screw the ledger strip to the side and bottom.

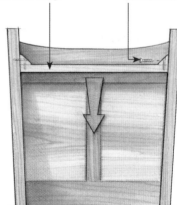

Fit and secure the bottom. The ledger strips have pairs of holes: One is for screwing the strip into the side of the chest and the other is for fixing the bottom in place.

Attach the lid. The author uses a strip of wood, clamped to the back of the chest, to help hold the lid in place while he secures the hinges.

sides to hold the hangers and then glue and clamp the hangers into their grooves. To make the openings for the tray handles, I used a shopmade template and a router equipped with a guide bushing and ¼-in. straight bit. First I marked the cutouts and removed the waste, just outside the line, with a jigsaw. Then I clamped the template on the tray and routed to the line, removed the template, and hit the edges with a ¼-in. roundover bit to soften them.

Ledger strips hold the bottom in place

Because the sides and ends of the chest angle in, the frame-and-panel bottom must be fitted from the bottom and then secured with a ledger strip from underneath. I drilled and countersunk for pairs of screws in the ledger strips. There's a little trial and error as you sneak up on the fit of the bottom. Keep in mind that a small decrease in width and length allows the bottom to take a large jump up into the chest.

Apply finish and add a rope stay

I finished the lid and bottom before attaching them to the chest. The interior and tray got a couple coats of Zinnser® Bulls Eye® clear shellac, cut with equal parts of denatured alcohol. For the outside, both sides of the top, and the battens, I wiped on a mixture of equal parts tung oil, satin spar varnish, and thinner. When the finish was dry, I attached the battens, remounted the lid, and secured the bottom.

For the rope stay, I found a Web site (www.animatedknots.com) that showed me, step by step, how to create an eye in the end of a line. I positioned the eye straps and rope so that the straps clear each other when the lid is closed and the open lid rests just a bit past vertical.

Shaker Chest of Drawers

CHRISTIAN BECKSVOORT

Years ago, clients wanted me to make a blanket chest to store shirts and sweaters. Blanket chests are great for quilts and blankets, but they tend to allow small items to drift toward the bottom and get lost. For clothes, I mused, drawers would make the contents more accessible. And if I used the same outside dimensions as a blanket box, they could still place the chest at the foot of the bed and sit on it, or push it against the wall to use as a dresser. The different drawer depths would add to the versatility of what the chest could hold. They took my advice and they still love the finished chest.

As with much of my work, this design is heavily influenced by the Shaker design ethic, with its simple lines, functional design, solid construction, and cherry wood. There are a number of parts, but the construction is straightforward. I use half-blind dovetails to secure the sides to a subtop, and a sliding dovetail to secure the bottom to the sides. A vertical divider gets centered in the top and bottom and dadoed in place. Front and back rails are notched around the vertical divider and dovetailed into place. I use a sturdy frame-and-panel back, glued into a rabbet, so the piece looks beautiful from all directions. And the main top gets screwed in place from the underside of the subtop. This is the same construction I use on all my case pieces, so the anatomy could work for a taller chest, too.

Tackle the sides first

Most of the business happens on the side pieces. But before I hand-chop any half-blind dovetails, the side pieces get a rabbet, leg arches, a sliding dovetail, and a dado with a dovetail at the front.

(continued on p. 28)

Dual-purpose jig for dadoes and dovetails. Like many chests of drawers, the sides of this one need a dovetail–dado combo for the rails and drawer runners and a long sliding dovetail for the bottom. One simple jig handles them all. Setup is easy. Registering off the front edge of the side, it's easy to clamp the jig square and cut dadoes and dovetails precisely.

Dovetail meets dado. Use a ¾-in. dovetail bit to cut the dovetail notch for the front and back rails (left). Without moving the jig (the author has two identical routers so he doesn't have to change bits), use a ¾-in. straight bit to cut the dado that will hold the drawer runners (right).

Two cuts for a long sliding dovetail. Before the final pass with a ¾-in. dovetail bit, the author uses a smaller straight bit to waste away the material, making the dovetail cleaner and easier to cut.

Built to Last

Half-blind dovetails, sliding dovetails, and dadoes ensure decades of flawless function. A frame-and-panel back makes the chest look good from all directions.

A. STRETCHER END DETAIL

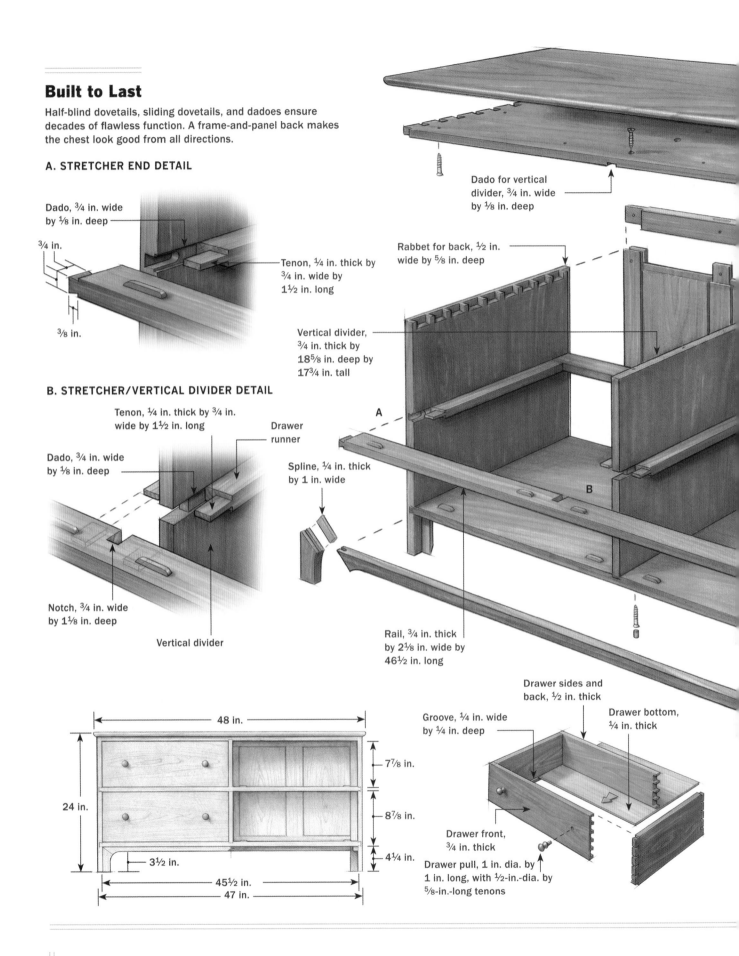

Dado, ³⁄₄ in. wide by ¹⁄₈ in. deep

³⁄₄ in.

³⁄₈ in.

Tenon, ¹⁄₄ in. thick by ³⁄₄ in. wide by 1¹⁄₂ in. long

B. STRETCHER/VERTICAL DIVIDER DETAIL

Tenon, ¹⁄₄ in. thick by ³⁄₄ in. wide by 1¹⁄₂ in. long

Dado, ³⁄₄ in. wide by ¹⁄₈ in. deep

Drawer runner

Notch, ³⁄₄ in. wide by 1¹⁄₈ in. deep

Vertical divider

Dado for vertical divider, ³⁄₄ in. wide by ¹⁄₈ in. deep

Rabbet for back, ¹⁄₂ in. wide by ⁵⁄₈ in. deep

Vertical divider, ³⁄₄ in. thick by 18⁵⁄₈ in. deep by 17³⁄₄ in. tall

A

B

Spline, ¹⁄₄ in. thick by 1 in. wide

Rail, ³⁄₄ in. thick by 2¹⁄₈ in. wide by 46¹⁄₂ in. long

48 in.

24 in.

3¹⁄₂ in.

45¹⁄₂ in.

47 in.

7⁷⁄₈ in.

8⁷⁄₈ in.

4¹⁄₄ in.

Drawer sides and back, ¹⁄₂ in. thick

Drawer bottom, ¹⁄₄ in. thick

Groove, ¹⁄₄ in. wide by ¹⁄₄ in. deep

Drawer front, ³⁄₄ in. thick

Drawer pull, 1 in. dia. by 1 in. long, with ¹⁄₂-in.-dia. by ⁵⁄₈-in.-long tenons

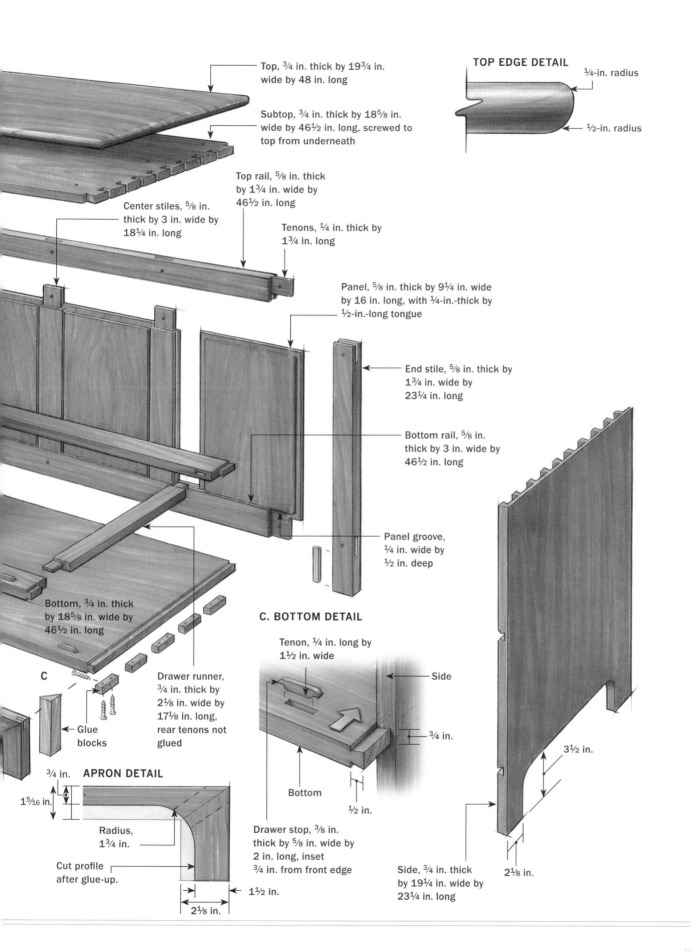

Top, ¾ in. thick by 19¾ in. wide by 48 in. long

Subtop, ¾ in. thick by 18⅝ in. wide by 46½ in. long, screwed to top from underneath

Top rail, ⅝ in. thick by 1¾ in. wide by 46½ in. long

Center stiles, ⅝ in. thick by 3 in. wide by 18¼ in. long

Tenons, ¼ in. thick by 1¾ in. long

Panel, ⅝ in. thick by 9¼ in. wide by 16 in. long, with ¼-in.-thick by ½-in.-long tongue

End stile, ⅝ in. thick by 1¾ in. wide by 23¼ in. long

Bottom rail, ⅝ in. thick by 3 in. wide by 46½ in. long

Panel groove, ¼ in. wide by ½ in. deep

Bottom, ¾ in. thick by 18⅝ in. wide by 46½ in. long

C

Glue blocks

Drawer runner, ¾ in. thick by 2⅛ in. wide by 17⅛ in. long, rear tenons not glued

TOP EDGE DETAIL

¼-in. radius

½-in. radius

C. BOTTOM DETAIL

Tenon, ¼ in. long by 1½ in. wide

Side

¾ in.

Bottom

½ in.

Drawer stop, ⅜ in. thick by ⅝ in. wide by 2 in. long, inset ¾ in. from front edge

3½ in.

Side, ¾ in. thick by 19¼ in. wide by 23¼ in. long

2⅛ in.

APRON DETAIL

¾ in.

1⁵⁄₁₆ in.

Radius, 1¾ in.

Cut profile after glue-up.

1½ in.

2⅛ in.

First, rabbet the side pieces with two ripcuts on the tablesaw. This rabbet will accept the back. Then draw the leg arches on the side pieces and use a bandsaw to cut them out and a block plane to smooth the straight edges. I clean up the arches using a balloon sander on my lathe and finish up with hand-sanding.

Now it's time to pick up the router and tackle the dovetail–dado that holds the front and back rails and the drawer runners as well as the sliding dovetail that holds the bottom. For all three I use a shopmade jig with two parallel bars, spaced the width of the router base, clamping it square to the carcase side. The same jig works for the dadoes on the sides of the vertical divider and the dadoes in the subtop and bottom that hold the vertical divider. While the router and jig are out, cut the dadoes in each side of the vertical divider. Along with the dadoes in the sides, these will hold the drawer runners. Line them up with the dadoes on the sides but leave the piece a bit long until you glue up the carcase and get an exact measurement.

Half-blind dovetails in large panels. Half-blind dovetails make a strong but clean-looking case. They can be a challenge on big pieces, but the author has tricks for keeping the pieces flat and aligned. On the subtop, the author marks the centers of the pins and uses a dovetail guide to lay out the tails (top left). To saw the long, wide board, he rests it on the floor and secures it in a vise. A thick, straight hardwood board clamped near the action keeps the wide board flat (above).

Chop and pare, chop and pare. Keeping the wide workpiece flat, make a vertical cut in the scribed line, tipping the chisel slightly forward (top right). Make the first cut light. Then, paring horizontally in from the end grain, remove a chip (above). Alternate between cutting down and cutting in until about halfway through, then turn the board over and repeat the process until you've met in the middle. Follow the same procedure after sawing the pins.

Nail down the tail board to mark pins. Mark the location of the tails on the pin board. On long, wide workpieces, the author uses a small nail to help in the transfer. Align the boards and predrill. Tap in the nail partway so it can be easily removed (top left). Using a marking knife and working from the nailed corner, scribe the tails onto the pin board (bottom left). Pivot the tail board into alignment whenever necessary.

Dovetailing a large case piece

Cutting dovetails on a large piece is very similar to cutting dovetails on a smaller box or drawer, but there are a few more things to consider. Holding the pieces is more challenging, keeping them flat is important, and of course there is more material to remove. The good news, at least with this piece, is that even if your dovetails don't look perfect, they'll be hidden by the subtop. I always lay out and cut the tails first, then transfer them and finish up with the pins.

Once you have the dovetails cut, it's time to glue the subtop to the sides. But first rout the dadoes for the vertical divider in the subtop and bottom (using the same jig as before). To find the center of both, it isn't necessary to do a dry-fit. The subtop, the bottom piece, and the rails are all the same length, so just stack the top and bottom together with the ends flush and measure for the center. After routing the dadoes, glue the dovetailed subtop to the sides. The bottom doesn't go in yet, so use spacers at the bottom of the legs to keep everything straight and square.

Cut the pins and then glue the top and sides. Spacers between the legs keep the assembly square while the author attaches the subtop to the sides. To keep from marring the carcase with heavy bar clamps, he uses spacers on the top and cauls on the sides.

How to Tame Long Sliding Dovetails

Long sliding dovetails can bind and freeze during assembly, but not if you follow the author's steps closely.

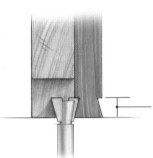

— ½ in.

While that assembly is drying, move to the router table to cut the sliding dovetails in the ends of the bottom and front and back rails. Then slide the bottom into place. I glued only the last 3 in. to 4 in. at the front of the sliding dovetail. Because the dovetail slot is deep, it weakens the sides of the case, so I added five glue blocks underneath each side. This strengthens and anchors the lower sections of the case sides to the bottom, yet still allows for wood movement.

Divider helps drawers run smoothly

The four drawers are separated by a vertical divider that is cut to fit after the case is assembled. With a handsaw, notch the vertical divider to accept the notched front and back rails, and then slide it in place. These notches line up with the dadoes that are already in the vertical divider. Don't glue the vertical divider in place because it is an end-grain to long-grain joint, and glue won't hold. Instead, screw it in place, plugging the holes in the bottom. The holes in the subtop will be covered by the top.

The bottom drawers run on the bottom of the case, but the top drawers run on a frame: two rails and four drawer runners. The runners are tenoned into the front and back rails. The tenons get glued into the front rail but are left loose in the back rail to allow for wood movement.

Finish panels before gluing in frames

A frame-and-panel back, although more work, gives as much diagonal racking resistance as plywood (unlike nailed shiplapped, tongue-and-groove boards) and looks much better. Once the case and all the dividers are in place, make the frame-and-panel back, leaving it a little too wide so you can sneak up on the perfect fit with a block plane. I profile the four panels with a 22½° panel-raising bit. I pin the rails and stiles for extra support and a nice design detail. Then I sand the inside face and fit

Big workpiece is an added challenge. A featherboard applies even pressure, keeping the long board on track and the cut precise. Go for a snug fit.

Please don't freeze. To prevent binding, don't use glue yet, and keep the bottom as straight as possible as you slide it in most of the way (left). Glue only the front 3 in. to 4 in. of the bottom (above); otherwise, the joint will seize while you are trying to bring the piece home. Use clamps to pull the bottom evenly and steadily. Clamping blocks that extend over the side keep the workpieces from getting damaged and, more important, stop the bottom when it is exactly flush with the sides.

the back to the case. I glue the back in place, secure it with small brads, countersink them, and plug the holes.

Complete the base and profile the top

To finish the front of the case, miter and spline the three-piece base assembly, bandsaw the arches to the same radius as the sides, and glue it into place. A one-piece base would introduce cross-grain gluing and could self-destruct. This way, the base expands and contracts (up and down), while the case side it is glued to does not change in length.

Next, sand the entire case and then cut the top of the case to size, allowing a ½-in. overhang on the front and on each side. Rout the profile into the front and sides, sand the top, and screw it into place from underneath through the subtop.

Rails and Dividers Guide the Drawers

This simple system keeps drawers from racking back and forth, tipping up, or dropping down.

1. Fit the vertical divider and tap it into position without glue. Screw it in from the top and bottom.
2. Fit the front rail and glue it into the sides and onto the vertical divider panel.
3. Install the four drawer runners. Apply glue only to the front tenons.
4. The back rail is glued into the dovetail slots and onto the vertical divider. The back mortise-and-tenon joints are not glued. This allows the web frame to telescope in and out as the case expands and contracts.
5. Fit the back. The end stiles extend beyond the bottom rail and become an integral part of the back legs. Use a block plane to sneak up on the fit before clamping and gluing.
6. Apply the mitered front base assembly. Add glue blocks afterward to strengthen the corner joints.

Drawers are the final step

Before starting the dovetails on the drawers, groove the sides and front. Now lay out the tails, saw and chop them, and move on to the pins. I cut the pins and tails slightly proud and flush everything up with a belt sander after the drawers are glued. Knob holes also can be drilled at this point. I use a pencil to mark the tight spots and a belt sander to remove material as I carefully fit the drawers to their openings.

Insert the drawer bottoms, and hold them in place with two saw slots and round-head screws in the underside of the drawer backs. The knobs are turned on the lathe, the tenons cut to length, and then glued into place.

Before applying a finish, I go over the entire piece to break and sand all edges including around the drawer openings, and the gaps between the frames and panels on the back. Then I sign the piece and give it three coats of an oil finish. The first coat is straight Danish oil, and the final two coats are a mixture of Tried & True™ varnish oil and spar varnish.

Classic Storage Cupboard

CHRISTIAN BECKSVOORT

In "Shaker Chest of Drawers" (p. 24), I wrote about a low chest of drawers and focused on its case construction, drawer runner system, and using a shopmade jig and router to cut dadoes and dovetail slots in the carcase. Since then, a client asked me to build a large cupboard to use in a kitchen.

This piece (and this chapter) picks up where "Shaker Chest of Drawers" left off. I'll expand on how I approach Shaker casework, showing you how to apply the three-sided face frame to the front. I'll also walk you through how I fit and install drawers. Also, because the drawers are so wide, I included a simple but effective center guide that keeps big drawers from binding.

The way I approached the doors is appropriate for almost any Shaker piece, so the editors gave that technique its own spotlight (see "Frame-and-Panel Doors Made Easier" on p. 42). By the way, because this piece will live in a kitchen, I sized the drawers to hold cutlery, kitchen linens, and even pots and pans. But this classic storage piece can be adapted to any room of the house. That's what the Shakers would have done.

Large panels can be a challenge

Other than the size of the panels, the carcase construction on this piece is almost the same as the low chest in "Shaker Chest of Drawers." There are a few differences: Because of the size of the pieces, I used a jigsaw instead of a bandsaw to cut the arches into the bottoms of the two sides. This chest has a permanent middle shelf that the low chest doesn't, and also because of the size of the pieces, I got creative about dovetailing and how I transferred the tails to the pin boards. I laid out and cut the tails first on the subtop, then moved to the half-blind pins on the sides. I rested the long workpieces on the ground and tacked the top in place with a small brad, creating a freestanding inverted U. I stood on a stool to transfer the tails to the pin board, and then cut the pins at the bench. Once the dovetails, dadoes, and rabbets were cut, I glued the subtop and bottom to the sides.

With the carcase together, it's time to work on the web frames and runners that will hold the drawers in place and allow them to run smoothly. For step-by-step details on this, see "Rails and Dividers Guide the Drawers," p. 32. To separate the top drawers, I added a centered vertical drawer divider and behind that a center runner. Although the three wide drawers at the bottom get an added center guide, don't tackle that until you've glued the frames in place and made the drawers.

(continued on p. 39)

Cupboard Details

The subtop and fixed shelf are cut back to accommodate the face frame and back assembly. The middle shelf also acts as a stop for the lower edges of the doors.

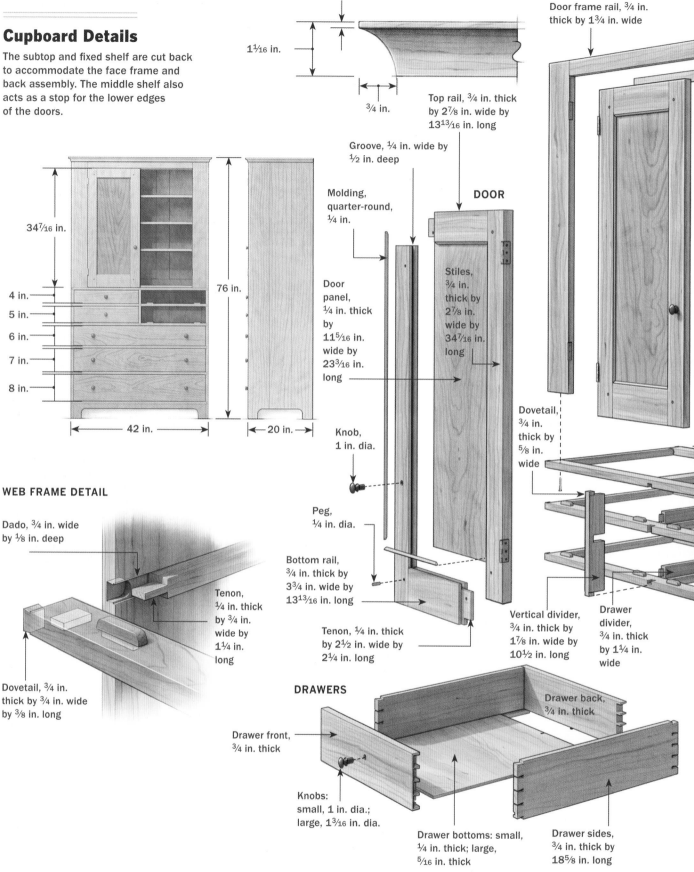

TOP DETAIL

¼ in.

1¹⁄₁₆ in.

¾ in.

Door frame rail, ¾ in. thick by 1¾ in. wide

Top rail, ¾ in. thick by 2⅞ in. wide by 13¹³⁄₁₆ in. long

Groove, ¼ in. wide by ½ in. deep

Molding, quarter-round, ¼ in.

DOOR

Door panel, ¼ in. thick by 11⁵⁄₁₆ in. wide by 23³⁄₁₆ in. long

Stiles, ¾ in. thick by 2⅞ in. wide by 34⁷⁄₁₆ in. long

34⁷⁄₁₆ in.

4 in.
5 in.
6 in.
7 in.
8 in.

76 in.

42 in.

20 in.

Knob, 1 in. dia.

Peg, ¼ in. dia.

Dovetail, ¾ in. thick by ⅝ in. wide

WEB FRAME DETAIL

Dado, ¾ in. wide by ⅛ in. deep

Tenon, ¼ in. thick by ¾ in. wide by 1¼ in. long

Dovetail, ¾ in. thick by ¾ in. wide by ⅜ in. long

Bottom rail, ¾ in. thick by 3¾ in. wide by 13¹³⁄₁₆ in. long

Tenon, ¼ in. thick by 2½ in. wide by 2¼ in. long

Vertical divider, ¾ in. thick by 1⅞ in. wide by 10½ in. long

Drawer divider, ¾ in. thick by 1¼ in. wide

DRAWERS

Drawer front, ¾ in. thick

Drawer back, ¾ in. thick

Knobs: small, 1 in. dia.; large, 1³⁄₁₆ in. dia.

Drawer bottoms: small, ¼ in. thick; large, ⁵⁄₁₆ in. thick

Drawer sides, ¾ in. thick by 18⅝ in. long

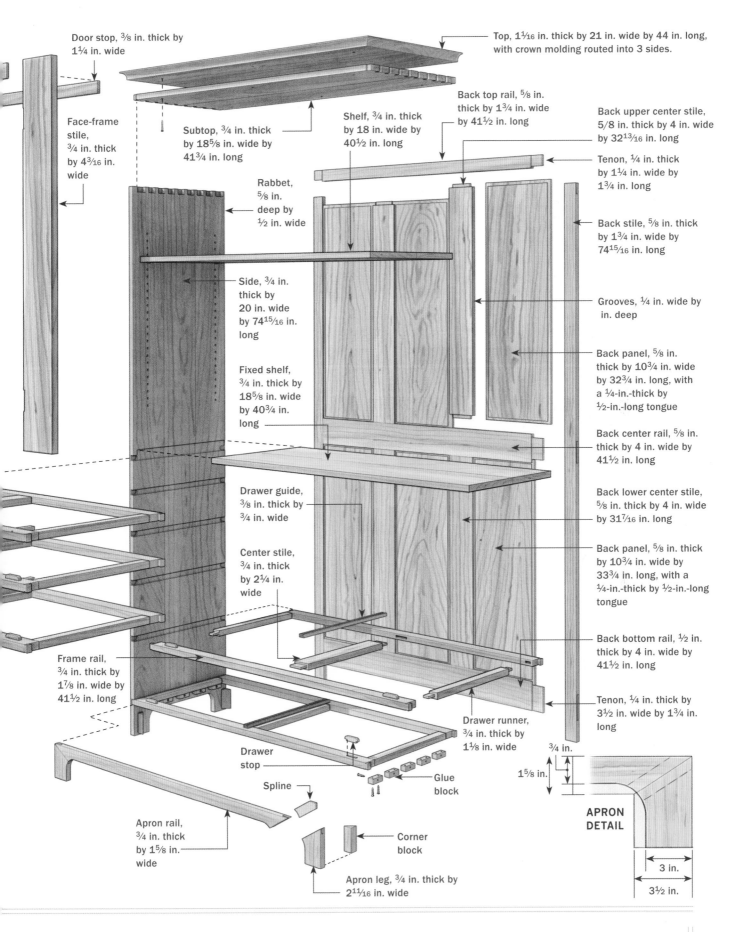

Door stop, 3/8 in. thick by 1 1/4 in. wide

Top, 1 1/16 in. thick by 21 in. wide by 44 in. long, with crown molding routed into 3 sides.

Face-frame stile, 3/4 in. thick by 4 3/16 in. wide

Subtop, 3/4 in. thick by 18 5/8 in. wide by 41 3/4 in. long

Shelf, 3/4 in. thick by 18 in. wide by 40 1/2 in. long

Back top rail, 5/8 in. thick by 1 3/4 in. wide by 41 1/2 in. long

Back upper center stile, 5/8 in. thick by 4 in. wide by 32 13/16 in. long

Tenon, 1/4 in. thick by 1 1/4 in. wide by 1 3/4 in. long

Rabbet, 5/8 in. deep by 1/2 in. wide

Back stile, 5/8 in. thick by 1 3/4 in. wide by 74 15/16 in. long

Side, 3/4 in. thick by 20 in. wide by 74 15/16 in. long

Grooves, 1/4 in. wide by in. deep

Fixed shelf, 3/4 in. thick by 18 5/8 in. wide by 40 3/4 in. long

Back panel, 5/8 in. thick by 10 3/4 in. wide by 32 3/4 in. long, with a 1/4-in.-thick by 1/2-in.-long tongue

Back center rail, 5/8 in. thick by 4 in. wide by 41 1/2 in. long

Drawer guide, 3/8 in. thick by 3/4 in. wide

Back lower center stile, 5/8 in. thick by 4 in. wide by 31 7/16 in. long

Center stile, 3/4 in. thick by 2 1/4 in. wide

Back panel, 5/8 in. thick by 10 3/4 in. wide by 33 3/4 in. long, with a 1/4-in.-thick by 1/2-in.-long tongue

Frame rail, 3/4 in. thick by 1 7/8 in. wide by 41 1/2 in. long

Back bottom rail, 1/2 in. thick by 4 in. wide by 41 1/2 in. long

Drawer runner, 3/4 in. thick by 1 1/8 in. wide

Tenon, 1/4 in. thick by 3 1/2 in. wide by 1 3/4 in. long

Drawer stop

Glue block

Spline

3/4 in.

1 5/8 in.

APRON DETAIL

Apron rail, 3/4 in. thick by 1 5/8 in. wide

Corner block

Apron leg, 3/4 in. thick by 2 11/16 in. wide

3 in.

3 1/2 in.

Make a solid face frame. Mortise-and-tenon joints add strength and simplify assembly: One clamp will hold it together. Gluing the frame into the case makes it completely rigid.

Inset it. The face frame goes inside the sides of the piece, but overlays the subtop, which is cut short to accommodate it. Make the frame just a bit larger than the opening, and trim the side pieces with a block plane to perfect the final fit. Apply clamp pressure from top to bottom, front to back, and along the sides.

Add the middle shelf and back. The fixed middle shelf (left) sits on the web frame below it, sharing a wide dado in the case sides. A dab of glue at the front and a finish nail through the top drawer frame hold it in place. Keep the clamps on the face frame or allow the glue to dry completely before adding the middle shelf. A frame-and-panel back (above) adds rigidity and racking resistance. Fit it and glue it into the rabbeted sides.

U-shaped face frame is applied

Once the rails and runners are in place, make the face frame for the upper half of the cabinet. You can do one of two things: Use an applied face frame that butts against the inside edges of the sides or use a more complicated approach that involves notching or mitering the side pieces on just the upper portion. I use the first, less complicated method, which leaves the edge of the cabinet sides exposed all the way to the top. This requires careful wood selection to hide the glue joint where the outsides of the frame meet the sides of the carcase but saves time and effort because you don't have to notch the carcase sides halfway or cut a stopped miter on the sides and miter the face frames.

When the frame is glued in place, sand the entire face of the cabinet flush. Then glue the fixed middle shelf into place, sliding it in from the back and against the face frame.

The back comes next. Because the back is captured in rabbets on the sides, I used 1¾-in.-wide quartersawn cherry for the side stiles and the top rail. The bottom and center rails as well as the center stiles can be flat-sawn and wider, for strength. The six panels are flat and flush inside and out. Use a block plane to carefully fit the back so that it just drops into the rabbet, and glue it in. Now you can make and fit the doors (see p. 42).

How to fit wide drawers. Careful fitting and smart stops are the key to good-looking drawers and a flush front. Size the front to the opening. Leave a small gap at the top edge to allow for wood expansion. Then cut the dovetails and assemble the drawer box.

Fit them individually. Start by rough-sanding the pins flush and get the drawer to just fit the opening (right). As you pull out the drawer, make pencil lines where the sides rub and use those lines as a guide to sand or plane the sides to an exact fit (above).

Add stops for a flush front. All the drawers get a stop at both ends. Use a trim router resting on the front edge of the drawer frames to cut shallow, 1¾-in.-long by ⅜-in.-wide grooves (left) for handmade stops. Then glue and clamp the stops into the grooves (right).

Wrap up some details, then tackle the drawers

With the doors complete, most of the hard parts are finished. While the case is still open, use a handheld drill and jig (a simple piece of plywood with predrilled holes) to drill holes on both sides of the upper section to accept pins for the adjustable shelves. Then glue in the mitered, splined apron in the base at the front.

Once the case is sanded, cut the top to size and then run a cove profile around the front and sides of the top on the router table. Screw it to the subtop from the inside.

Drawers are the last hurdle and the most time-consuming. I cut half-blind dovetails in the front and through-dovetails in the back, and I always cut the tails first. On the tablesaw, groove the front and the two sides for the drawer bottoms. These grooves will help align things when it's time to transfer the tail layout to the pin boards. On the wide drawers, make sure to locate the grooves ¾ in. from the bottom to allow enough room for the center track.

After you complete the drawers, turn the knobs, glue them in place, and add drawer stops to the fronts of the web frames. Next,

make the tracks for the wide drawers to run on. They are fitted, centered, and glued and screwed to the front and center rails. Now drill a hole and insert a dowel into the drawer back, centered exactly. Finally, test-fit each drawer and make adjustments.

I finished the case with Tried & True Danish oil. Once dry, I screwed in the drawer bottoms, polished the brass hinges, and added leather bumpers to the door and drawer stops.

Center Guides Keep Them in Line

Wide drawers have a tendency to bind, but this simple dowel system keeps them running smoothly.

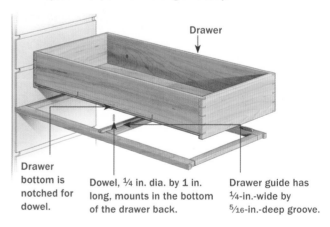

Drawer

Drawer bottom is notched for dowel.

Dowel, ¼ in. dia. by 1 in. long, mounts in the bottom of the drawer back.

Drawer guide has ¼-in.-wide by 5⁄16-in.-deep groove.

Make a groovy center strip. The center guide is simply a piece of wood with a groove that runs straight through.

Center a dowel on the drawer bottom. The author measures for the center to lock in the location and uses a doweling jig to drill straight.

Use a stick to keep it on track. To keep the guide centered as you mark around it, use a notched stick at the front and then the back. Glue and screw the guide only to the front and back rails of the web frames.

Frame-and-Panel Doors Made Easier

CHRISTIAN BECKSVOORT

I make Shaker doors differently from the way others do. While you can't beat a mortised-and-tenoned, pegged frame for strength and style, I prefer a thin, inset panel surrounded by a quarter-round molding as opposed to raised-panel or pillowed-panel doors. Although the Shakers used moldings sparingly, the quarter-round along the inner edges of the frame makes for a clean, slightly rounded, and understated design. This style can blend into both period and modern environments.

The second difference is that I apply the molding, rather than cutting it into the frame parts. The flat, inset panels are only ¼ in. thick in a ¾-in. frame, leaving room for the quarter-round molding around the inside edge. I apply the moldings because it's tedious and tricky to cope or miter the profiled frame. And if you mess it up, you have to go back and remake the part, which not only means time lost but also could jeopardize a nice grain pattern you've already chosen. Also, the anatomy of a molded frame is much more complex. By the way, Shaker furniture makers occasionally applied these moldings, too.

Traditional Method is Difficult

When the molding is part of the frame, it makes the joinery complex. You have to cut away part of the stile, and cope or miter the molding for a clean joint.

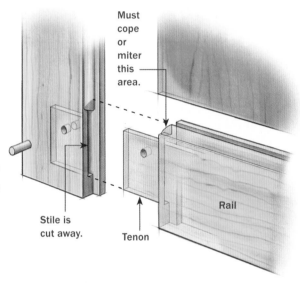

Must cope or miter this area.

Stile is cut away.

Tenon

Rail

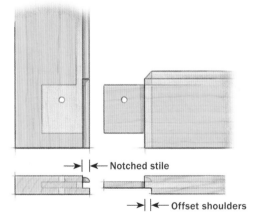

→| |← Notched stile

→| |← Offset shoulders

42

A Better Way: Add Molding after Assembly

Applying the molding after the fact allows you to have a simpler mortise-and-tenon joint, with even shoulders.

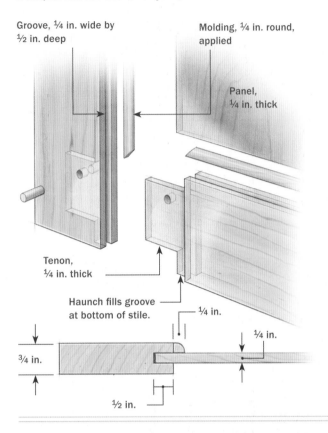

Groove, ¼ in. wide by ½ in. deep

Molding, ¼ in. round, applied

Panel, ¼ in. thick

Tenon, ¼ in. thick

Haunch fills groove at bottom of stile.

¼ in.

¼ in.

¾ in.

½ in.

Start with a solid frame. The author recommends a full mortise and tenon. A single peg in each corner adds a decorative element and ensures that the joint stays strong. He finishes the panel beforehand.

Cut the molding. A wide workpiece is easier and safer to machine. Cut the quarter-round profile on the router table (profile both sides of the piece) and then rip the moldings to width on the tablesaw.

Fit it piece by piece. Glue the molding to the frame only, not to the panel. Work on one piece at a time, marking, cutting miters, and gluing as you go. Use hand pressure to keep the pieces in place for about 1 minute each and then leave a few pieces of tape behind as clamps.

Cut the Molding

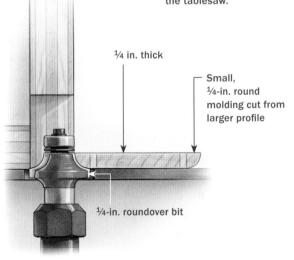

¼ in. thick

Small, ¼-in. round molding cut from larger profile

¼-in. roundover bit

Fit the length first. If the door isn't parallel to the case, you'll have to make an angled cut. Working on one door at a time, butt the door to the hinge side and mark the door parallel to the bottom of the opening.

Making the doors

I try to use quartersawn stock to minimize the gaps created by seasonal movement between the door panels and face frame. Cut the four stiles ⅛ in. longer than the opening and the four rails, then cut the grooves on the inside edges of all the parts on the tablesaw. Using a router or drill press followed by a mortise chisel, cut the mortises. Then cut the tenons on the tablesaw, leaving a ½-in. haunch to fill the exposed grooves, top and bottom. Next, cut the bookmatched door panels to size, sand them, and test the fit. Before gluing the doors together, I oil the panels so no raw wood shows if they shrink in dry months. Glue and pin the joints, and sand both faces.

Now I simply cut, fit, and glue the ¼-in. quarter-round moldings to the outside face of the frame, all the way around the panel. Then I fit the doors to the opening.

Getting the doors to fit the case

Start with a slightly oversize door and work on the length first, then the width. Working on one door at a time, butt the first door to the hinge side of the opening. Things can be very slightly out of square. This isn't a problem. If the bottom of the door isn't square to the case, mark it and square it on the jointer. Then, because the top of the opening might not be parallel to the bottom, do the same thing to the top of the door. Once the bottoms and tops of both doors match the case, take off enough material to leave a ¹⁄₁₆-in. gap on the top and ⅛ in. on the bottom. This technique also works for a single door.

Jointer Handles Straight and Tapered Cuts

You can't run the entire end of the door over the jointer because the end grain on the trailing edge will blow out. The author's technique prevents that. And he uses a time-tested trick for tapered cuts.

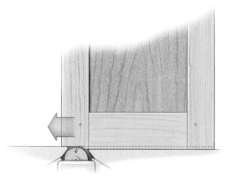

FOR A STRAIGHT CUT
First, with the cut set to the final depth, feed the leading end just a bit.

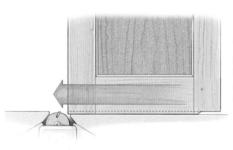

Then reverse the door so the first cut is on the trailing end. Run the door straight through to complete the cut.

A jointer speeds door-fitting. Begin by getting the top and bottom to fit in the opening. One or both may not be parallel to the case or each other, but the jointer gets them to fit perfectly whether you have to cut a straight line or a taper.

FOR A TAPERED CUT
First make a leading-end cut (same as for a straight cut) to the maximum depth of the taper. Then reverse the door, pivoting the uncut end down onto the outfeed table.

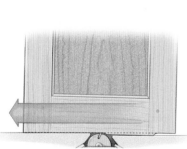

Run the door through the jointer to finish the cut. Presto, perfect taper.

Use a trim router for hinge mortises.
Hinging can be daunting, but a trim router does the grunt work and ensures a perfectly uniform depth. A small router is easier to balance on narrow edges.

Mortise the doors first. First, mark for the hinge mortise. The hinges line up with the top and bottom rails. Hold the hinge in place and trace around it lightly with a knife. Then remove the hinge and cut heavier lines to rout to and place the chisel in later.

Clamp the doors together. Two doors create a wider base for the router (above) and you can cut both mortises at once. If you only have one door, clamp another board flush for a wider base. Pivot the bit down into the cutting area to get started and work close to the lines, cleaning up with a chisel (left).

Then mortise the case. To start, transfer the location to the carcase. Once the hinges are screwed to the doors, position them in the opening, leaving the gap you want along the top and bottom edges. Use a marking knife to transfer the hinge placement; then remove the door (and unscrew the hinges), set the hinges in place on the edge of the frame, and mark around them.

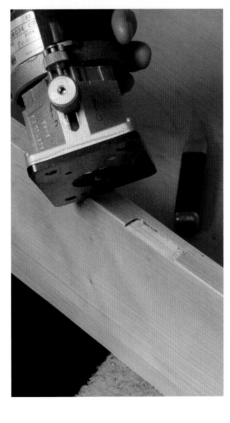

Rout the face frame. Rout close to the layout lines again and finish with a chisel. Then check the fit on the knob side of the door, or between doors if there are two. Remove the door(s), trim that final edge, and then reinstall the door(s). You should have perfect gaps all around.

To fit the width of the doors, set both doors in place and trim them (on the jointer) so they just fit into the opening with about a 1/16-in. gap at the hinges. The final fitting will be done after the hinges are in. Last, drill for the doorknobs and add brass butt hinges on both doors.

Chimney Cupboard

MICHAEL PEKOVICH

One of the great things about Shaker furniture is that no two pieces are exactly alike. Aside from chairs, the Shakers didn't make furniture for commercial production. Each piece was essentially a one-off design, made for a specific purpose or even an individual user, so the variations are endless. And in spite of the restrained design sense, there is a playful, subtle originality to each piece. It's what inspires me to make furniture in the style and to make it my own.

I'd wanted to make a chimney cupboard for a while because I like the tall, slender proportions of the form. Every original example I've seen, though, has just a pair of doors, one stacked on the other. Wider cupboards, on the other hand, typically have an arrangement of drawers at waist height that add interest and utility. I like that look so I figured, Why not sneak a few drawers into my chimney cupboard? The result, in keeping with the Shaker spirit, is an original design in the classic vernacular.

Construction is simple yet solid

I looked to the Shakers for the anatomy too but chose elements that are as straightforward as possible. Most of the joints are rabbets and dadoes. There are just a few half-blind dovetails at the top where the subtop rails connect to the case, but they're hidden, so there's no need to stress there either. Dressing up the

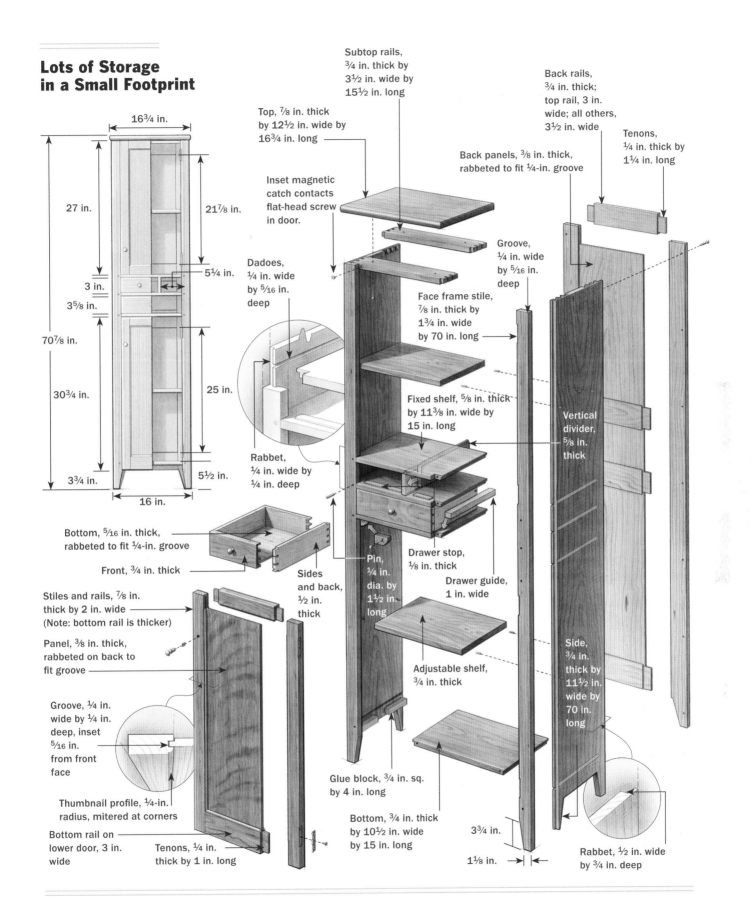

Lots of Storage in a Small Footprint

16¾ in.

27 in.

21⅞ in.

5¼ in.

3 in.

3⅝ in.

70⅞ in.

25 in.

30¾ in.

3¾ in.

5½ in.

16 in.

Subtop rails, ¾ in. thick by 3½ in. wide by 15½ in. long

Top, ⅞ in. thick by 12½ in. wide by 16¾ in. long

Inset magnetic catch contacts flat-head screw in door.

Back rails, ¾ in. thick; top rail, 3 in. wide; all others, 3½ in. wide

Back panels, ⅜ in. thick, rabbeted to fit ¼-in. groove

Tenons, ¼ in. thick by 1¼ in. long

Dadoes, ¼ in. wide by 5⁄16 in. deep

Groove, ¼ in. wide by 5⁄16 in. deep

Face frame stile, ⅞ in. thick by 1¾ in. wide by 70 in. long

Fixed shelf, ⅝ in. thick by 11⅜ in. wide by 15 in. long

Vertical divider, ⅝ in. thick

Rabbet, ¼ in. wide by ¼ in. deep

Bottom, 5⁄16 in. thick, rabbeted to fit ¼-in. groove

Front, ¾ in. thick

Sides and back, ½ in. thick

Pin, ¼ in. dia. by 1½ in. long

Drawer stop, ⅛ in. thick

Drawer guide, 1 in. wide

Stiles and rails, ⅞ in. thick by 2 in. wide (Note: bottom rail is thicker)

Panel, ⅜ in. thick, rabbeted on back to fit groove

Groove, ¼ in. wide by ¼ in. deep, inset 5⁄16 in. from front face

Thumbnail profile, ¼-in. radius, mitered at corners

Bottom rail on lower door, 3 in. wide

Tenons, ¼ in. thick by 1 in. long

Adjustable shelf, ¾ in. thick

Glue block, ¾ in. sq. by 4 in. long

Bottom, ¾ in. thick by 10½ in. wide by 15 in. long

Side, ¾ in. thick by 11½ in. wide by 70 in. long

3¾ in.

1⅛ in.

Rabbet, ½ in. wide by ¾ in. deep

Simple Dadoes and Rabbets

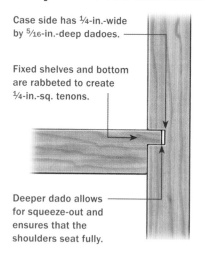

Case side has ¼-in.-wide by ⁵⁄₁₆-in.-deep dadoes.

Fixed shelves and bottom are rabbeted to create ¼-in.-sq. tenons.

Deeper dado allows for squeeze-out and ensures that the shoulders seat fully.

Accurate dadoes at the tablesaw. Clamp a long hook stop to your crosscut sled to position the case sides (inset). Dado both sides before moving the stop for the next pair of dadoes. The extra plywood on the sled base creates zero clearance around the dado blades.

Add an end stop for the bottom dado. Screw the stop to the sled (above). Hold-down clamps secure the case side and prevent it from lifting or pivoting during the cut (right).

Rabbet the shelves to fit. Widen the dado set to ⅜ in. and bury a portion of the blade in a sacrificial fence to dial in the width of the rabbet. Use a featherboard to ensure a consistent depth. Aim for a snug fit and fine-tune the joint with a shoulder plane.

front is a partial face frame, really just a pair of stiles glued to the sides. The stiles hide the shelf dadoes, but they also allow an opportunity to peg the case to the shelves for added strength. The primary wood is cherry, but I used pine for the frame-and-panel back. The back adds rigidity and the pine lightens up the look of the interior. Finishing things off is a top with a subtle bullnose profile. It overhangs the front and sides and is attached to a pair of subtop rails. The rails add rigidity to the top and also act as a door-stop. I simply glued and screwed on the top because the grain of all the parts runs in the same direction and seasonal movement isn't an issue.

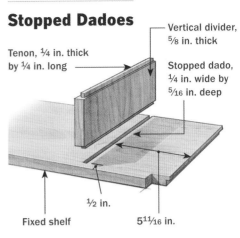

Vertical divider,
⅝ in. thick

Tenon, ¼ in. thick
by ¼ in. long

Stopped dado,
¼ in. wide by
⁵⁄₁₆ in. deep

½ in.

Fixed shelf

5¹¹⁄₁₆ in.

Stopped dadoes for the vertical divider. Clamp both shelves together with the back edges adjacent. Rout the dadoes using a straightedge to guide the router base. Stop short of the ends and square up the dadoes with a chisel.

Glue blocks under the bottom shelf and drawer blocks at the center shelves lend additional support. Added up, this is a very fast and strong way to build a cabinet.

This project is also a good one for working entirely by hand, but for that I'd probably do the whole thing in pine.

How to work efficiently

Though most of the joinery is simple dadoes, there are a lot of them, so I came up with ways to make the process as efficient as possible. First I cut the dadoes narrower than the shelves, dividers, and bottom and then rabbeted those parts to fit.

This approach has some big benefits. First, rabbeting a part to fit a dado is much easier than milling a part to a precise thickness to fit a full-width dado. Second, the rabbet creates a shoulder on the shelf that registers against the inside face of the case side. This makes for much more accurate glue-ups because it doesn't rely on the bottom of the dado being perfectly even (which is difficult

to pull off on a wide case side). And because the joint registers off the shoulder, you can cut the dado a little deep, which allows room for excess glue to gather and prevents squeeze-out. The face frame and back panel hide any gap at the bottom of the joint.

To cut the dadoes for the shelves, dividers, and case bottom, I used a crosscut sled and a ¼-in.-wide dado blade on the tablesaw. To cut the three dadoes for the shelf and drawer dividers, I registered the work against a long hook stop (see the photos on the facing page). The dado for the case bottom is a little trickier because the long side can pivot during the cut. For that dado, I made a stop block with hold-down clamps and attached it to the sled.

While I had the ¼-in.-wide blade in the saw, I grooved the back of the face-frame stiles. The trick here is to locate the groove so that the face frame will be about ¹⁄₃₂ in. proud of the case side when glued up, so you can plane the face frame flush to the case. If you're really organized, you can cut the panel grooves in the door and back frame parts

Rout and chop the waste. A router makes quick work of removing most of the stock. The author reground a pair of chisels at an angle to work into the corners as he chops the end grain. Afterward, he pares to the scribe line with a wide chisel, as shown.

Dovetails strengthen the top. Scribe the case sides. A shallow rabbet on the inside face of the rails (above) makes it easier to align the parts for scribing (right).

now as well. I hate changing out my dado blade more than I have to. One more thing: You can use cutoffs from the grooved parts to dial in a perfect fit on the rabbets later.

Next, I widened the dado set and rabbeted the case sides, dividers, and shelves. The case sides get a rabbet along the back and front edges. The rabbet in the back houses the case back. The one at the front creates a tongue that fits the groove in the back of the face frame stiles. It's a little more work than simply butting the parts together, but the tongue-and-groove joint makes it easier to register the parts during glue-up and can help correct any slight bow in the long case sides.

The two horizontal dividers require a stopped dado to accommodate the vertical drawer divider. I handled this with a router. Clamp both shelves to the workbench. With a T-square fence clamped in place, you can rout both shelves at once, saving time and ensuring perfect alignment.

Dovetails lock the top of the case

The subtop rails are joined to the case sides with half-blind dovetails. Start by cutting the tails on the subtop rails and then transfer their layout to the case sides. I normally stand the pins board in a vise for scribing, but the sides for this case were too long for that. Instead, I placed the side flat on the benchtop and held the rail vertically while scribing and then I kept them right there to rout, chop, and pare away the waste.

The last task before assembly is to cut out the feet on the case sides and the bottom of the face-frame stiles.

Start with the face frame. Shape the feet first. The author jigsaws the profile on the case sides and then smooths it with a block plane, using a file to work into the corners. He tapers the bottom of the face frame on the bandsaw, smoothing the cuts with a bench plane.

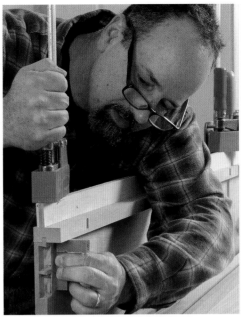

Glue the face frame to the case sides.
A narrow caul directs pressure over the joint and distributes it along the length. Check for square during clamping. When the glue is dry, plane the face frame flush to the case sides.

Notch the shelves. The fixed shelf and dividers end up flush with the case front, so they need to be notched to fit around the face frame. Butt them against the face frame and be sure they are vertical when scribing. Cut outside the line and pare to fit with a chisel.

Face frame anchors everything else

Normally the face frame is the last thing I add when building a case, but it's the first thing I tackled on this project. Gluing the stiles to the sides first eased construction in a couple of ways. First, it allowed me to plane the stiles flush while the side assemblies were easy to deal with; doing it when the whole cabinet is together is awkward. It also was easier to mark and notch the shelves to fit around the stiles at this stage. And that let me assemble the rest of the case all at once, without having to slide in the shelves afterward.

The case bottom and the front subtop rail butt against the back of the face frame and act as door stops. The fixed shelf and dividers, on the other hand, end up flush with the front of the face frame, so you need to notch them to fit around it. With the stiles already glued to the case side, it's easy to scribe the

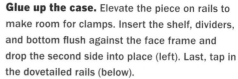

Glue up the case. Elevate the piece on rails to make room for clamps. Insert the shelf, dividers, and bottom flush against the face frame and drop the second side into place (left). Last, tap in the dovetailed rails (below).

Add the vertical divider. Plane its neighbors, then slide it in. (1) Go slowly when planing to avoid gouging the face frame. (2) Then slide the vertical divider most of the way in, apply glue, and tap it home. (3) Plane the divider flush when the glue is dry.

notches. Mark them a little high, so the shelves end up protruding a bit from the front of the case. That will let you plane them perfectly flush later. Cut just outside the line with a handsaw or on the bandsaw and pare the remaining waste with a chisel.

Assembly continues with gluing up the sides, shelves, and bottom and top rails. Dry-

fit and clamp the parts together and check for square. This is also a good time to check that all the shelf notches are sized properly. A notch that's too narrow will look fine from the front of the case, but won't allow the shelf to seat fully. Also the notch should be deep enough so that when slid forward, the shelf

The Top Gets a Bullnose

Chamfer, ¼ in. wide by ⅛ in. deep

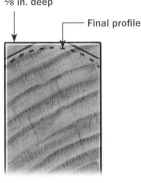

Final profile

Profile is plane easy. Lay out pencil lines as a guide and plane a wide, shallow chamfer along each edge (left). Then plane off the peaks for a smooth curve. Keep the corners crisp (right) for a nice shadow line.

Attach the top and back. The top can be glued and screwed directly to the subtop rails because the grain on the parts is running in the same direction (left). Trim the frame-and-panel back to a snug fit and screw it in place (above).

or divider is just proud of the face frame. When everything looks good, go ahead and glue up the case. Once all the clamps are on, add the glue blocks under the bottom shelf. Apply a thin coat of glue on two faces and rub the block back and forth until it grabs. The vacuum will hold it in place without clamps. To allow for seasonal movement, apply multiple short blocks along the joint rather than one long one. The drawer guides are glued in the same way, but because the guides are long, glue the front half only. Afterward, drill through the face frame at the shelf, divider, and bottom locations and pin the joints. This really locks the assembly and adds a little visual interest.

Safe Slotting on the Bandsaw

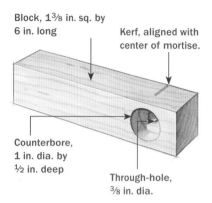

Block, 1³⁄₈ in. sq. by 6 in. long

Kerf, aligned with center of mortise.

Counterbore, 1 in. dia. by ½ in. deep

Through-hole, ³⁄₈ in. dia.

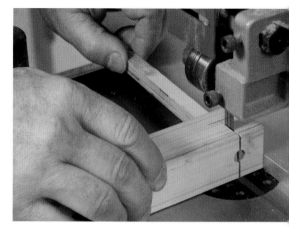

A simple block holds the pull. Insert the pull into the stepped hole (left) and slide the block along the rip fence into the cut (right). Stop ¹⁄₁₆ in. short of the pull's shoulder.

A jig for wedges, too. A scrap of medium-density fiberboard (MDF) with an angled notch makes quick work of wedges (above). To install the drawer pulls, add glue to the mortise and insert the pull. Press in the wedge (right), tap it home, and trim flush.

After the case has dried, flush up the shelf and dividers with the face frame. Then slide the vertical divider in place, and plane it flush. All that's left of the case work is to glue the top in place and add the frame-and-panel back. The back has two center rails aligned with the fixed shelf and lower divider, allowing you to screw the back to them as well as the sides, further strengthening the case joinery.

Doors and drawers are straightforward

The doors are classic Shaker: simple flat panels surrounded by a thumbnail profile. I like to rout the profile into the door frame and miter it where the parts meet. But Christian Becksvoort offers a simpler alternative (see "Frame-and-Panel Doors Made Easier," on p. 42). He makes a standard frame-and-panel door and adds a quarter-round molding to the inside edge of the frame after assembly.

A Hidden Wedge for Doors

For a clean look on the inside of the doors, the author hides the wedge in a stopped mortise. The wedge is placed into the slot before installing the pull.

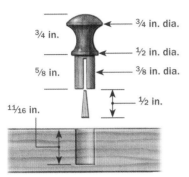

¾ in.

5/8 in.

11/16 in.

¾ in. dia.

½ in. dia.

3/8 in. dia.

½ in.

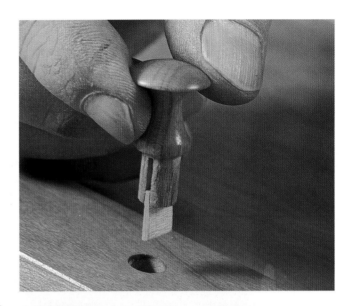

Self-setting. Insert the wedge into the slot (top) and then install the pull. Use a pine block as a pad when driving in the pull (above). As the wedge contacts the bottom of the mortise, it is forced into the slot, expanding the tenon for a tight fit.

The drawers are traditional dovetail construction. The important thing is to cut all the fronts from a single board for a continuous grain match. I turned my own pulls, but if you don't have a lathe, you're not out of luck. Hardwood knobs are readily available. They're typically a little clunky, but it's easy to refine the profile on the drill press.

The pulls on the doors and drawers are secured with wedges. For the drawers, I simply drilled a hole through the drawer front and wedged the pull from the inside. On the door, I got a little fancier. I didn't want the tenon exposed on the inside of the door but I still wanted to wedge it. So I used a really cool joint called a fox-wedged tenon. You start by drilling a stopped mortise. Then you insert a wedge into the kerf in the tenon and insert the pull into the mortise. If everything is sized correctly, the wedge contacts the bottom of the mortise, forcing it into the kerf as you drive in the pull, creating a self-wedging joint. The only trick is to cut the wedge to the right length so that the pull seats before the wedge bottoms out in the kerf. Wedging is simple in concept but tricky in practice. The toughest part is kerfing the tenons of the pulls. Cutting kerfs in such small, odd-

shaped parts can be difficult, but a simple block makes it easy on the bandsaw. You can use the same block to cut the tenons to length.

I finished the case and knobs before installing them. It makes for less nooks and crannies to work around when finishing. I used a wiping varnish, building it up for a deep luster and good protection, followed by steel wool and wax.

Pennsylvania Spice Box

STEVE LATTA

When I decided to build a piece to celebrate my tenth wedding anniversary, I had two important goals. I wanted it to be on an intimate scale and I wanted a piece that could be personalized.

This spice box seemed a perfect fit. It's compact enough to sit on a dresser or in an alcove, and it's great for storing jewelry and small treasures of all kinds.

This design is typical of those popular among Pennsylvania Quakers throughout the 18th century. Fitted with banks of small drawers and often hidden compartments, they were displayed as symbols of prosperity. The cases typically were made of walnut, the doors or central drawers veneered or inlaid with combinations of maple, boxwood, holly, cherry, walnut burl, locust, and red cedar.

Dovetailing the carcase. Rabbeting the dovetails makes it easier to lay out the pins and also makes the tails easier to hide with moldings. Clamp a wooden fence onto the router to make the rabbets.

Bury the bit. Pivot the fence into the bit to create a zero-clearance cavity that thwarts tearout. Adjust the fence to cut rabbets of varying depths with a single ¾-in. bit.

Transfer the layout. Mark the appropriate corners of the top and bottom panels (left) and cut them to fit into the side rabbets. Then scribe the pin layouts (right).

An Array of Tabs and Dovetails

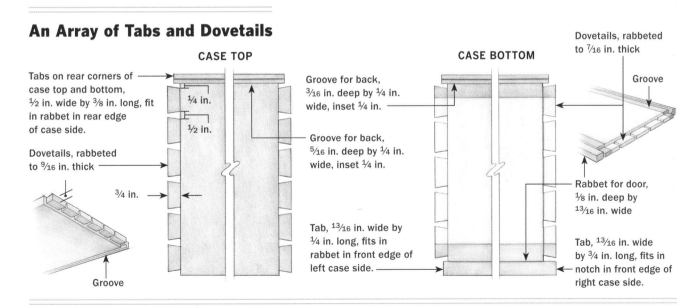

CASE TOP

Tabs on rear corners of case top and bottom, ½ in. wide by ⅜ in. long, fit in rabbet in rear edge of case side.

Dovetails, rabbeted to ⁹⁄₁₆ in. thick

¾ in.

Groove

¼ in.

½ in.

Groove for back, ³⁄₁₆ in. deep by ¼ in. wide, inset ¼ in.

Groove for back, ⁵⁄₁₆ in. deep by ¼ in. wide, inset ¼ in.

Tab, ¹³⁄₁₆ in. wide by ¼ in. long, fits in rabbet in front edge of left case side.

CASE BOTTOM

Dovetails, rabbeted to ⁷⁄₁₆ in. thick

Groove

Rabbet for door, ⅛ in. deep by ¹³⁄₁₆ in. wide

Tab, ¹³⁄₁₆ in. wide by ¾ in. long, fits in notch in front edge of right case side.

An Intricate Treasure Chest

The box houses 11 dovetailed drawers with veneered fronts, and two secret compartments. The case, door, and trim are from a single walnut board. The bottom and interior partitions are poplar, glued up with a walnut strip at the front; the back is ash. Hardware is from Londonderry Brasses (www.londonderry-brasses.com).

ASYMMETRICAL CASE SIDES

The case sides look very different up front. The door rests in a rabbet on the left side and overlaps a cutout on the right to swing out of the way of the drawers.

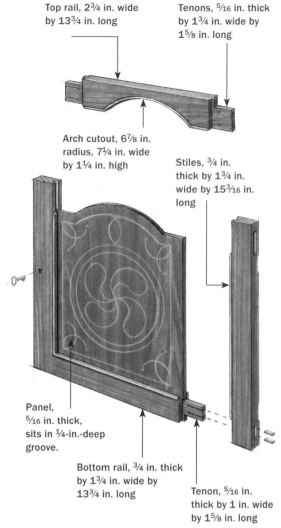

Top rail, 2¾ in. wide by 13¾ in. long

Tenons, ⁵⁄₁₆ in. thick by 1¾ in. wide by 1⅝ in. long

Arch cutout, 6⅞ in. radius, 7¼ in. wide by 1¼ in. high

Stiles, ¾ in. thick by 1¾ in. wide by 15³⁄₁₆ in. long

Panel, ⁵⁄₁₆ in. thick, sits in ¼-in.-deep groove.

Bottom rail, ¾ in. thick by 1¾ in. wide by 13¾ in. long

Tenon, ⁵⁄₁₆ in. thick by 1 in. wide by 1⅝ in. long

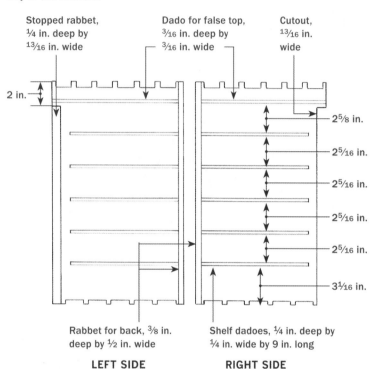

Stopped rabbet, ¼ in. deep by 13⁄₁₆ in. wide

Dado for false top, ³⁄₁₆ in. deep by ³⁄₁₆ in. wide

Cutout, 13⁄₁₆ in. wide

2 in.

2⅝ in.

2⁵⁄₁₆ in.

2⁵⁄₁₆ in.

2⁵⁄₁₆ in.

2⁵⁄₁₆ in.

3¹⁄₁₆ in.

Rabbet for back, ⅜ in. deep by ½ in. wide

Shelf dadoes, ¼ in. deep by ¼ in. wide by 9 in. long

LEFT SIDE   **RIGHT SIDE**

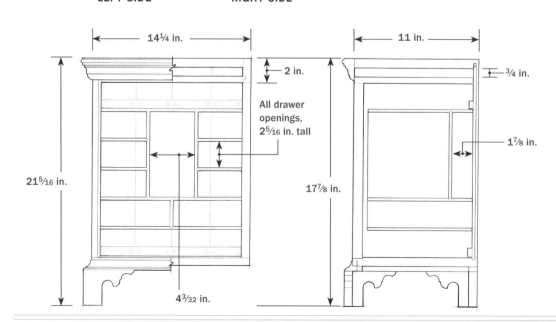

14¼ in.

2 in.

All drawer openings, 2⁵⁄₁₆ in. tall

21⁵⁄₁₆ in.

4³⁄₃₂ in.

11 in.

¾ in.

1⅞ in.

17⅞ in.

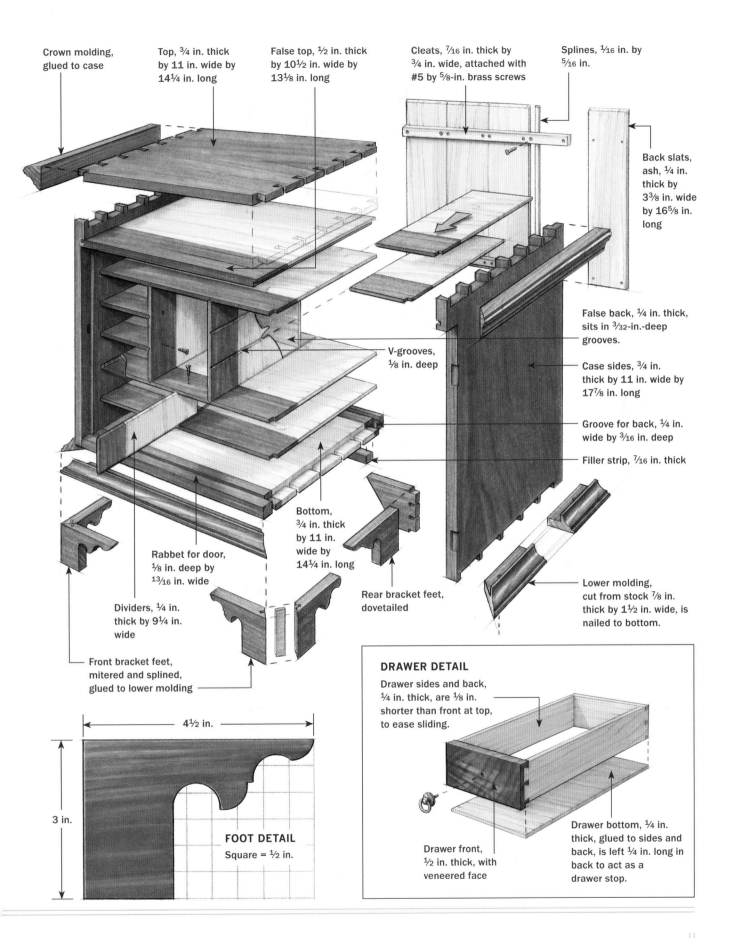

Crown molding, glued to case

Top, ¾ in. thick by 11 in. wide by 14¼ in. long

False top, ½ in. thick by 10½ in. wide by 13⅛ in. long

Cleats, ⁷⁄₁₆ in. thick by ¾ in. wide, attached with #5 by ⅝-in. brass screws

Splines, ¹⁄₁₆ in. by ⁵⁄₁₆ in.

Back slats, ash, ¼ in. thick by 3⅜ in. wide by 16⅝ in. long

V-grooves, ⅛ in. deep

False back, ¼ in. thick, sits in ³⁄₃₂-in.-deep grooves.

Case sides, ¾ in. thick by 11 in. wide by 17⅞ in. long

Groove for back, ¼ in. wide by ³⁄₁₆ in. deep

Filler strip, ⁷⁄₁₆ in. thick

Bottom, ¾ in. thick by 11 in. wide by 14¼ in. long

Rabbet for door, ⅛ in. deep by ¹³⁄₁₆ in. wide

Rear bracket feet, dovetailed

Lower molding, cut from stock ⅞ in. thick by 1½ in. wide, is nailed to bottom.

Dividers, ¼ in. thick by 9¼ in. wide

Front bracket feet, mitered and splined, glued to lower molding

FOOT DETAIL

Square = ½ in.

4½ in.

3 in.

DRAWER DETAIL

Drawer sides and back, ¼ in. thick, are ⅛ in. shorter than front at top, to ease sliding.

Drawer front, ½ in. thick, with veneered face

Drawer bottom, ¼ in. thick, glued to sides and back, is left ¼ in. long in back to act as a drawer stop.

Case assembly. For clean, precise stopped dadoes, build this jig. Its fence mates with the rabbet on the workpiece edge, preventing tearout at the entrance to each dado. A notch in the stop block prevents trapped sawdust from shortening the cut.

Picture of a calm glue-up. The author leaves the bottom dry-fit while gluing up the top, sparing himself the panic of getting the whole case together at once.

Start with the case joinery

The case is dovetailed and the various rabbets and notches for the door and the back complicate the joinery a little. Lay out and cut the dovetails (but not the pins yet), keeping in mind all those insets and rabbets. Next, mount a ½-in. or ¾-in. straight bit in a handheld router and bury the bit in a fence clamped to the base. Set the router to cut a rabbet that is ⅜ in. deep by ½ in. wide and use this setup to rabbet the rear, interior edges of both case sides. These rabbets will receive the back.

For the front of the case, you now need to cut a stopped rabbet on the interior of the left side. When closed, the lock side of the door will fill this recess, which should be ¼ in. deep by ¹³⁄₁₆ in. wide. Adjust your fence and bit depth, then cut the rabbet, stopping 2¹⁄₁₆ in. from the top. Don't square the rounded end of the rabbet just yet. The squared end should be trimmed flush with the bottom of the false top, so wait until you've fitted the false top before taking this step. On the hinge side, the door sits in a notch ¹³⁄₁₆ in. deep that stops 2¹⁄₁₆ in. from the top.

The next step with the router is to rabbet the dovetails. Reset the router fence to cut the length of the tails. For both pieces, be sure to rabbet only the dovetails, not the notches in front and back. Before transferring the tail layouts to the end grain of the pin boards, trim the tabs at the rear of the top and bottom pieces so they fit into the side rabbets for the back. Also trim the front tab on the bottom to fit in the left-side rabbet for the door (see the drawing on p. 59). Cut the pins.

Next, along the inside edges of the top and bottom, cut the grooves to receive the back panel. Cut the groove in the bottom ¼ in. wide by ³⁄₁₆ in. deep. The top groove should be slightly deeper—⁵⁄₁₆ in.—to facilitate the back panel sliding up and dropping into the bottom groove. This can be done with the router-and-fence setup or with a dado blade.

With that, all of the main carcase joinery is cut and the pieces are rabbeted and notched to accommodate a back and a door. But before glue-up, you need to start on the interior of the case.

Prep the case for the partitions

Inside the case, lightweight and delicately joined partitions create space for 11 drawers and two secret compartments. The first of these—a hidden file space ¾ in. deep—is created by a false top hidden behind the crown molding. The false top should be crosscut to length but left wide until after its joinery is cut. To hold it in the case, use a router to cut a through-dado in each case side, 1½ in. from the top. Crown molding will cover these. Using a dado blade buried in an auxiliary fence, cut a notch along the ends of the false top to fit into the dadoes.

The horizontal drawer dividers are joined to the cabinet sides with stopped dadoes ¼ in.

Partitions. Cut partition joinery on the router table. Set up a 90° V-groove bit to cut halfway through the stock's depth. The widest part of the groove should match the stock's thickness. Next, bury the bit in the fence to chamfer the mating ends, which should come to a point that is centered on the stock.

wide by ¼ in. deep. These dadoes should stop ⁵⁄₈ in. back from the front edge on the hinge side and the rabbet on the lock side. I cut these using a router jig that stops the cut and eliminates blowout along the back edge.

Once the dadoes are cut, glue up the case with the false top.

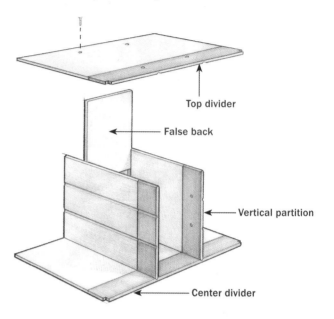

A preventive measure. The partition joinery will be secured in several places with wood screws. Before installing the partitions, predrill and countersink the screw holes to avoid splitting the stock.

Preassemble the Central Gallery

Because the false back is captured by grooves on all four sides, you must pre-assemble the central gallery and slide it into place in one piece.

Top divider

False back

Vertical partition

Center divider

Partitions slide in from the back. The author dry-fits the interior, fitting the pieces to one another, then removes and prefinishes the pieces before final assembly. Screws hold the assembly together.

Fitting the central partitions

The lightweight partitions are joined to each other with chamfered ends fitted precisely into shallow V-grooves. These V-joints, combined with the stopped dadoes, allow everything to be slid into the case from the back. The divider fronts are slightly rounded over and these roundovers meet seamlessly at the V-joints.

Leave the partitions wide until all of the notches, V-grooves, and front details are completed. Start by cutting the three main horizontal dividers to length. This dimension should be the side-to-side distance between shelf dado bottoms, minus 1/32 in. to make them slide easily. Next, cut V-grooves into the faces of these dividers to accept the vertical partitions that run between them. Use a 90° V-groove bit mounted in a router table, riding the partitions against the fence. The bottom of the V-groove should be exactly halfway through the stock. If you have a little flat at the groove bottom, use a chisel to bring it to a point.

Now slide the three dividers into their respective dadoes and measure for the length of the vertical partitions. When you cut these partitions to length, leave them a little long.

Next, bury the V-groove bit in the fence and set it to chamfer precisely halfway through the end of the partition stock. Chamfer the bottom and top edges of the vertical partitions to a point so they fit into the V-grooves in the three main panels. Slide the partitions into their slots and, using a straightedge, check whether the horizontal partitions are bowed. If so, shorten the verticals with a light pass of the block plane and rechamfer. A good fit is critical.

Each of the long vertical partitions now needs a pair of V-grooves to accept short horizontal dividers. Lay out the grooves to align with the side dadoes and cut them using the V-groove bit in the router table. Slide the partitions back into the case.

Determine the length of the short horizontal dividers by measuring from the bottom of the V-grooves to the bottom of the dadoes cut into the sides. Cut these dividers to length and chamfer the inside edges. Next, notch the ends of the horizontal partitions to fit over the ends of the stopped dadoes in the case sides. This creates a nice, clean termination of the partitions into the sides. Mark the notches with a chisel or knife and cut them with a handsaw and chisel.

Once everything fits, use a 5/16-in. roundover bit and a router/router-table setup to round the front edges of all of the partitions. Use only a small portion of the cutting edge to apply a shallow roundover. This makes for a really clean look.

You can now cut the partitions to width on the tablesaw.

Fit the hidden compartment

A small box, accessible only from the back of the case, fits behind the large central cavity. Consequently, a false back made from ash, the same material as the real back, needs to be fitted in that section. Using a 1/4-in. straight bit chucked into a handheld router with an auxiliary fence mounted to the base, cut a groove to receive the false back. It is cut on the inside faces of the two main vertical dividers and between the two V-grooves on the top two horizontal dividers. Size a cutoff from the back to fit into the recess.

Next, screw all of the partitions and dividers together using #3 or #4 by 5/8-in. wood screws. Predrill and countersink to avoid splitting. Small nails would work great also.

At this stage, you should have a box and its false top glued together. All of the internal dividers are dry-fitted and cut to the right depth, with their front edges nicely detailed.

Crown Molding

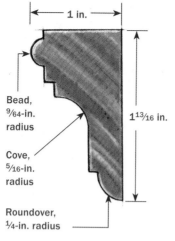

1 in.

Bead, 9/64-in. radius

Cove, 5/16-in. radius

Roundover, 1/4-in. radius

1 13/16 in.

Attach the crown molding. Cut a shallow V-groove along the molding's bottom edge to capture excess glue and reduce squeeze-out. Molding cutoffs serve as cauls to create a square clamping surface.

Base Molding

Cove, 9/16 in. radius

Rabbet, 7/16 in. by 3/4 in.

89°

7/16 in.

1 1/2 in.

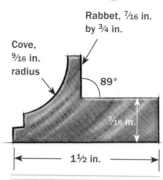

The cove molding is notched. The lip provides a nailing surface for attaching the molding from underneath. Make the first tablesaw cut a degree out of square for a snug fit against the case.

Making the back

The back is made from four 1/4-in.-thick ash slats with chamfered edges, splined and battened together. Cut a shallow groove, about 3/16 in. deep, in the edges where the boards meet, using a 1/16-in. tablesaw blade. After the panel is glued up, use a block plane to cut a chamfer along the inside of the top edge of the back panel. This chamfer allows you to lift and tip the back panel into position and then drop it into the lower groove.

Making the crown molding and feet

I copied the crown molding from an 18th-century box, using a shaper and a cutter I ground to match. The molding can also be made with a combination of router bits.

The cove molding at the bottom is made from stock measuring 7/8 in. thick by 1 1/2 in. wide. Using a cove cutter mounted in the router table, scallop out the top of the molding. Cut the fillet next, using a slot cutter

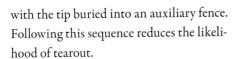

Bracket feet. The front feet are mitered. For glue-up, place a piece of 2-in. packing tape over the outside of the joint (top). Pretreat the end grain with a light layer of glue. After adding more glue and folding the miter together, insert the spline (above).

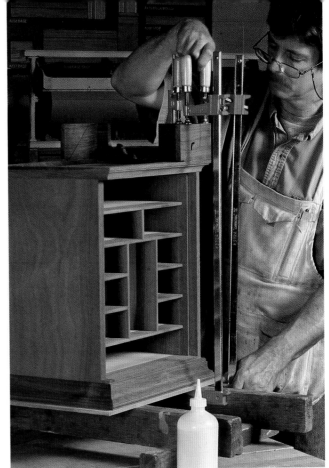

Clamp the assembly. The author uses a wide, double-wrapped rubber band to clamp the assembly. He uses the negative-image offcuts from the scrollsaw as cauls for gluing the feet to the cove molding.

with the tip buried into an auxiliary fence. Following this sequence reduces the likelihood of tearout.

This molding needs to be notched so that it covers the lower dovetails and lips underneath the case. Glue a filler piece measuring $\frac{7}{16}$ in. thick by 1 in. wide along the lower back edge of the case between the moldings. It provides a level surface for mounting the feet.

The flat bracket feet are made from $\frac{1}{2}$-in.- to $\frac{5}{8}$-in.-thick stock that's 3 in. wide. I prefer to use a straight grain that brings the eye to the center of the piece. The front feet are made from sequentially sawn pieces that are mitered and splined. Cut the groove for the spline on the tablesaw using a 45° block mounted to a miter gauge. Cut the spline

from $\frac{1}{8}$-in. stock whose grain runs parallel to the grain orientation in the feet. After the miter joint is cut, lay out the foot detail and cut it out on the scrollsaw. The rear feet are dovetailed. I broke from tradition and used primary wood for the rear return because the back of the chest would be visible. After the four foot glue-ups are dry, glue them to the lower cove molding, making them flush to its front edge.

Making the door

Mill the door stock in stages and leave the stiles and rails a couple of inches overlong and at least $\frac{1}{4}$ in. to $\frac{3}{8}$ in. extrawide, even after reaching final thickness of $\frac{3}{4}$ in. Cut the arch in the approximate center of the top stile. Lay out the curve and cut it with

Shopmade Beading Tool

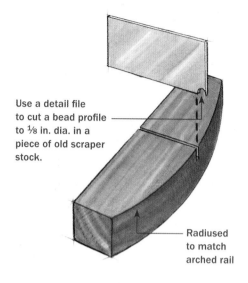

Use a detail file to cut a bead profile to ⅛ in. dia. in a piece of old scraper stock.

Radiused to match arched rail

Arched door. This scratch stock is built for curves. The block is shaped to match the radius of the door's arched top. Stop the bead short of the corner and clean it up with a chisel.

Miter the beaded corners. A simple cutting guide makes it easy to pare the corners cleanly at 45°.

a bandsaw; clean up the sawmarks with a card scraper.

The straight inside edges of the door frame are beaded first—on both the inside and outside faces. To cut the beads, I use my slicing gauge and define the inner line on all of the components; then I use a detail file to rough in the radius on the edges. I use a shopmade scratch stock to define the bead. With a white-lead pencil, mark what will be the top of the bead and scrape only until the lead disappears. This helps guarantee an even bead without too many high or low spots.

For the arched rail, bead the flats on both sides of the arch, being careful not to run all the way to the corners. Remount the scratch stock into a block of wood radiused to match the curve in the rail and bead the arches. Using a chisel, small knife, gouge, sandpaper, or other means, blend the corners together on the arched piece.

Once all the edges are beaded, cut the pieces to final length and width, keeping in mind that the door is oversize and will be taken to dimension later. Lay out and cut the 5/16-in. through-mortises, centered along

Sturdy frame for a picture-perfect panel. The door's inlaid panel slides into a frame joined with mortises and wedged through-tenons.

Revealing Hidden Compartments

Remove the bottom drawer and reach through the opening to slide the back upward. When it clears the lip of the lower groove, it tilts away from the bottom and out of its housing.

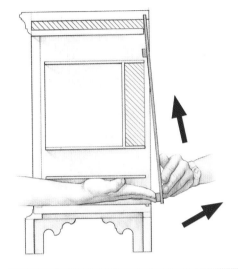

Hidden treasure. Both hidden compartments are accessed from the back of the box. The shallow space above the false top conceals documents. The deep box in the alcove can hold small valuables.

the thickness of the stock, leaving about $7/32$ in. on each side. Next, plow a $1/4$-in.-deep groove the same width as the mortise along the internal edge of the stiles and rails. I use a slot cutter on a router table, clamping on an auxiliary fence and making sure the tip of the cutter is buried in the fence where it would make contact with the stock. I shaped another auxiliary fence for the arched portion of the top rail, setting it up so it was also just $1/4$ in. deep.

I cut the tenons on the tablesaw and hand-pared the internal miters using a guide block. Because the groove is deeper than the $1/8$-in. bead, do a sample to figure out the quirks. The tenons need a $1/8$-in. haunch to fill the groove. Because it is such a small door, I did not bother angling the haunch in, as I would on larger doors. Cut the tenons for wedges and, with the door dry-fit, turn to the panel.

Once the inlay is done, glue up the door. Because of all the miters and the need to fuss

a little, use white glue and take advantage of its extra open time. With the door clamped, make sure it is flat, pound in the wedges, release the clamps, and let the door dry.

Size the door to the opening, mortise in the lock and hinges, and hang it in the case. I typically line up the hinges with the rails. To calculate the location of the lock mortise, use machinist's blue/white correction fluid on the end of the bolt. With the door closed, turn the key, forcing the bolt against the case side. Cut the mortise with a small chisel. To finish the case, door, and drawer fronts, I padded on several coats of garnet shellac.

The High Art of the Lowboy

PHILIP C. LOWE

The Queen Anne lowboy is about as traditional as American furniture gets, but from a modern perspective this 18th-century piece is still highly practical. The lowboy can be used as a dressing table or hall table, and the design has lost none of its elegance in the last 300 years.

For an intermediate woodworker looking to grow as a craftsman, the lowboy is an ideal project. It's not overly big or complex, but it is a satisfying, high-level test of many skills; so many, in fact, that you're almost guaranteed to learn one or two new ones before you're done. The piece combines a mortise-and-tenoned case with cabriole legs, dovetailed drawers, and a tabletop with a hand-shaped edge profile. A fan carving decorates the center drawer.

I've modified some of the period construction details to build a case that will accommodate seasonal wood movement. It's not an exact reproduction, but it captures the spirit of the early pieces.

Mahogany Lowboy

This small piece lets you develop your turning, joinery, and carving skills and learn how to apply an antique-looking finish.

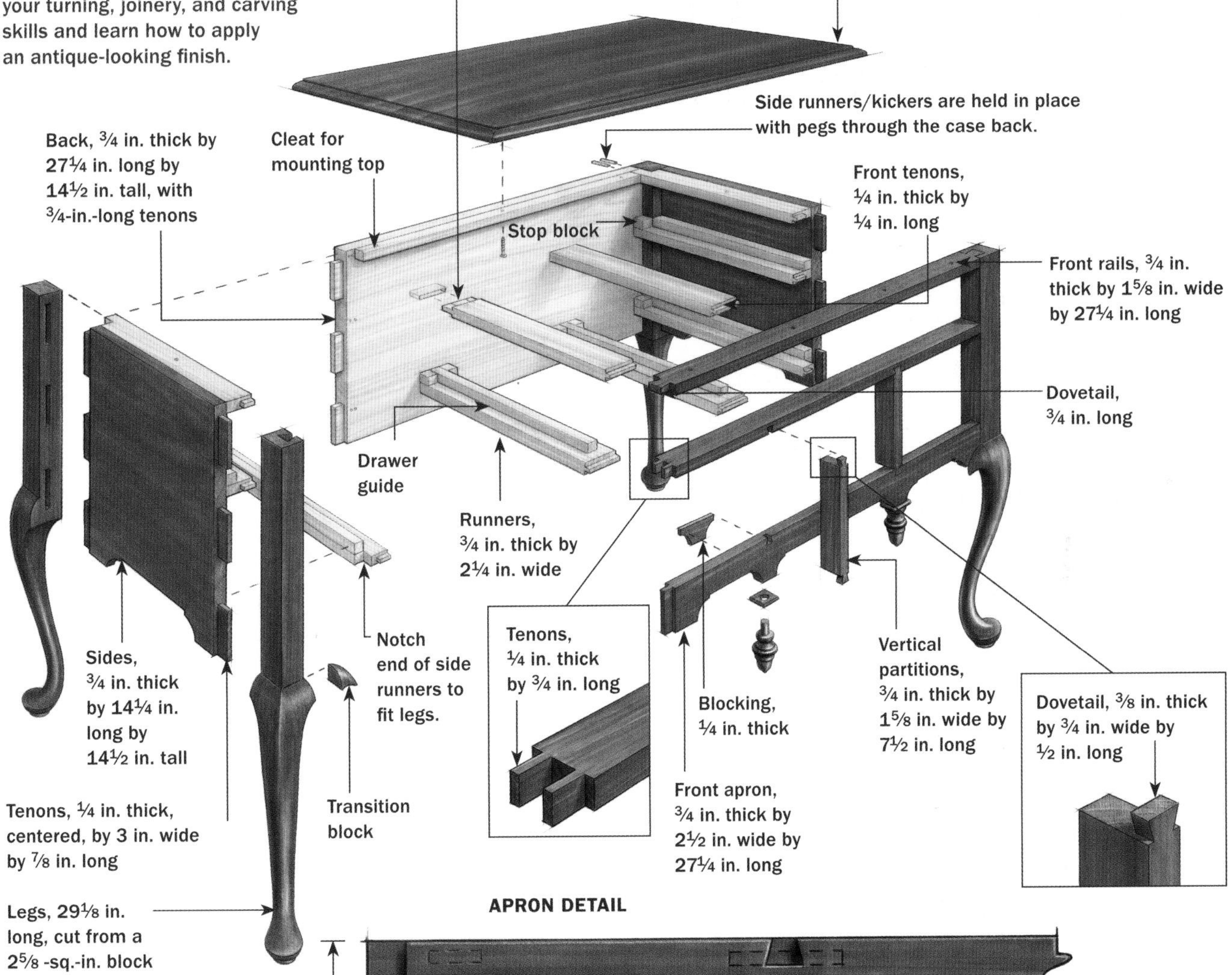

Center runners/kickers have 1/4-in.-thick by 3/4-in.-long tenons wedged through the back.
Top, 7/8 in. thick by 18 in. wide by 32 in. long
Side runners/kickers are held in place with pegs through the case back.
Back, 3/4 in. thick by 27 1/4 in. long by 14 1/2 in. tall, with 3/4-in.-long tenons
Cleat for mounting top
Stop block
Front tenons, 1/4 in. thick by 1/4 in. long
Front rails, 3/4 in. thick by 1 5/8 in. wide by 27 1/4 in. long
Dovetail, 3/4 in. long
Drawer guide
Runners, 3/4 in. thick by 2 1/4 in. wide
Sides, 3/4 in. thick by 14 1/4 in. long by 14 1/2 in. tall
Notch end of side runners to fit legs.
Tenons, 1/4 in. thick by 3/4 in. long
Blocking, 1/4 in. thick
Vertical partitions, 3/4 in. thick by 1 5/8 in. wide by 7 1/2 in. long
Dovetail, 3/8 in. thick by 3/4 in. wide by 1/2 in. long
Tenons, 1/4 in. thick, centered, by 3 in. wide by 7/8 in. long
Transition block
Front apron, 3/4 in. thick by 2 1/2 in. wide by 27 1/4 in. long
Legs, 29 1/8 in. long, cut from a 2 5/8 -sq.-in. block

APRON DETAIL

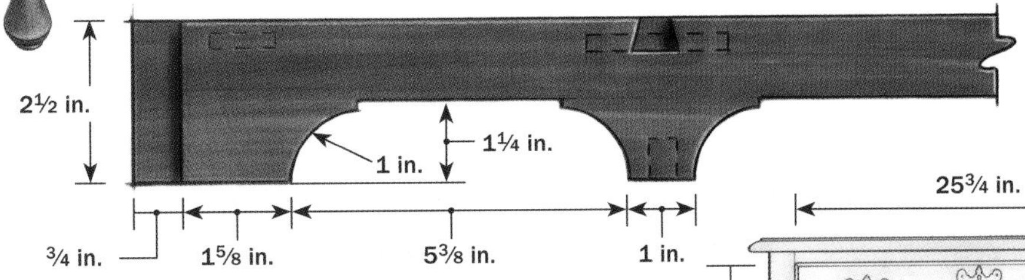

2 1/2 in.
1 in.
1 1/4 in.
3/4 in.
1 5/8 in.
5 3/8 in.
1 in.

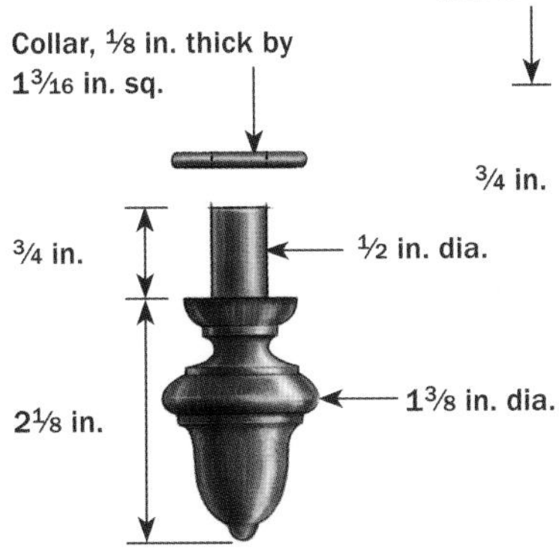

Collar, 1/8 in. thick by 1 3/16 in. sq.
3/4 in.
1/2 in. dia.
2 1/8 in.
1 3/8 in. dia.

DROP FINIAL

The pattern shown here is half size.

DRAWER DETAIL

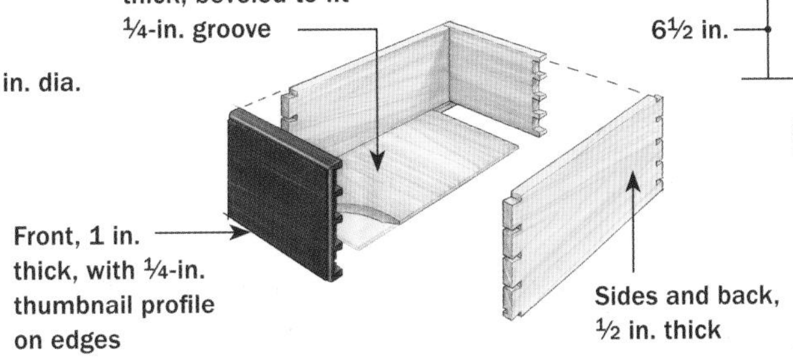

Bottom, 1/2 in. thick, beveled to fit 1/4-in. groove
Front, 1 in. thick, with 1/4-in. thumbnail profile on edges
Sides and back, 1/2 in. thick

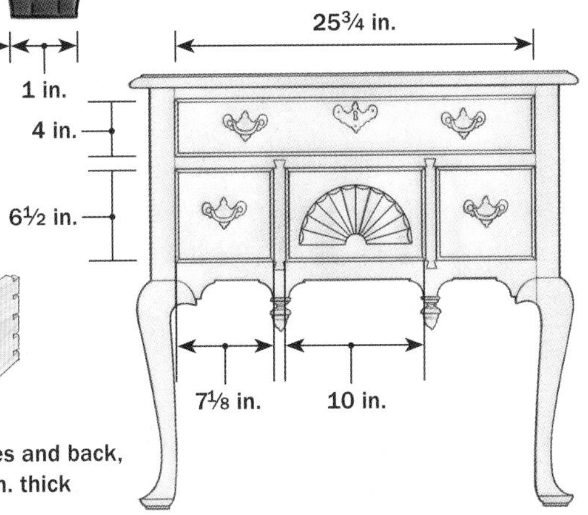

25 3/4 in.
4 in.
6 1/2 in.
7 1/8 in.
10 in.

Turn and Shape the Legs

The legs take shape in two distinct stages. Start by laying out and turning the pad foot. Then rough out the leg's overall shape at the bandsaw and refine it with chisel, rasp, file, and scraper.

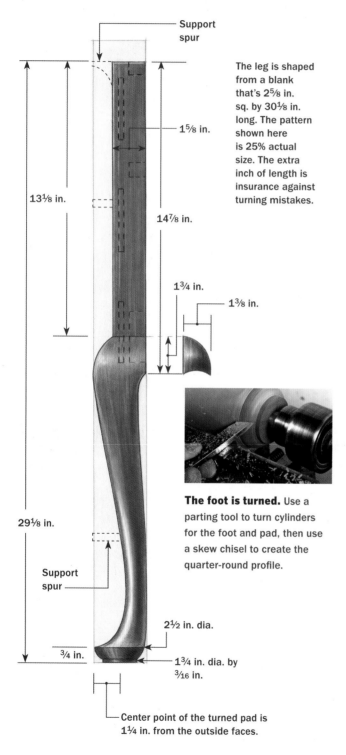

Support spur

The leg is shaped from a blank that's 2⅝ in. sq. by 30⅛ in. long. The pattern shown here is 25% actual size. The extra inch of length is insurance against turning mistakes.

1⅝ in.

13⅛ in.

14⅞ in.

1¾ in.

1⅜ in.

The foot is turned. Use a parting tool to turn cylinders for the foot and pad, then use a skew chisel to create the quarter-round profile.

29⅛ in.

Support spur

2½ in. dia.

¾ in.

1¾ in. dia. by 3/16 in.

Center point of the turned pad is 1¼ in. from the outside faces.

The cabriole leg: grace under pressure

These cabriole legs are slender but balanced and strong enough to support a heavy case piece without stretchers. They also do more than just hold the case off the floor; their long top posts are an integral part of the case itself. The case can't go together until the legs are done, so let's begin with the four legs.

It's most practical to turn the foot and cut the mortises before sawing and shaping the curved cabriole profile. The first step is to orient the leg blanks for the best figure. Mark the inside corners of each leg, then trace the cabriole pattern on these two adjacent surfaces. On each leg, use a cutting gauge to score a line defining the post block. Set the gauge to the dimension of the waste to be cut away. Score these lines on the tops of the legs, too; this helps keep the position of the leg clear.

To lay out the turned foot, scribe a line around the bottom of the blank to mark the top of the foot. Draw center marks on the two ends of the blank to locate the points of the lathe centers for the offset turning.

Turning and mortising

At the lathe, use a parting tool to turn a cylinder for the foot from the layout line to the end of the blank. Then turn a narrower cylinder at the very end of the blank to establish the pad at the bottom of the foot. Next, use the point of a turning skew to score a line where the square corners of the blank meet the cylinder, defining the top of the foot. Use the skew to soften the hard corners of the square and then shape the foot by rounding off the cylinder to a quarter-round. Sand the foot while it is on the lathe.

Each leg is mortised on the two inside faces to accommodate one case side and either the solid back or the front apron and rails.

Cut the curved profile.
Start cutting the profile by first defining the edge of the spurs. Then make cuts to complete the basic profile.

Rotate the blank and cut again. Save the cutoff with the pattern drawn on it and tape it back in place to guide this second cut. The spurs will steady the leg for these subsequent cuts.

Layout lines guide the shaping. Start with a centerline on each face, then split the distance from the centerline to the edge of the leg with a line that runs from the knee to the ankle.

Chamfer the corners to form an octagon.
Use a flat chisel. To stay with the grain, always work from the convex surfaces to the concave ones.

Shave away the remaining corners. Use a flat-soled spokeshave to cut a second, narrower set of chamfers, effectively rounding the leg.

Smooth the surface. Finish rounding the profile with a rasp and a smooth file.

Referencing from the top of each blank and factoring in the extra inch, use a combination square to mark the tops and bottoms of the mortises. Use a cutting gauge and reference from the inside corner of each blank to mark the fronts and backs of the mortises. Cut the mortises at the drill press or mortiser.

Saw and refine the shape

At the bandsaw, cut the leg's curved profile into one of the laid-out faces. Tape on the waste piece at the back of the leg and cut the other face. Be sure to save the long waste piece sawn from the post. You can use this material for transition blocks. Next, with the leg held in a bar clamp and vise, use a spokeshave to remove the bandsaw marks and smooth all four surfaces.

Trim the post. Dimension the post block with a pair of stopped cuts on the tablesaw. These cuts are made to the right and left of the fence so the inside corner of the post block is against the fence. The untrimmed waste just above the knee is removed after glue-up.

Lay out matching tenons. Clamp one of the front rails to the back panel and scribe the shoulder lines for both pieces simultaneously. Clamp the scribed rail to its mates and scribe shoulders on the remaining pieces.

Cut the joinery with a dado set. For consistency, cut face-side tenon cheeks on all of the pieces before adjusting the setup (if needed) to cut the opposite cheeks.

Mark out and cut the tenons. For the sides and back panel, you need to fashion multiple tenons from the full-width tongues. Hold each panel against its mating post and scribe the mortise locations on the tongue (above). Remove the waste with a coping saw and chisel (right), leaving a little room for the tenons to move in the top and middle mortises. This allows room for seasonal expansion of the sides and back toward the top. The transition blocks prevent downward expansion.

After cleaning up the cuts, finish shaping the leg by cutting a series of chamfers at the corners to round the profile. File the leg and scrape with a card scraper. Then trim the post blocks and cut the posts to length.

Precise joinery ensures a square case

Building the case is a challenge in precision. There are no steps or reveals to mask inaccuracies where the sides, back, or rails meet the corner posts. Everything is flush.

With the mortises already cut in the posts, the next step is to lay out and cut the tenons on all of the mating pieces. I begin with the back and the front rails. These pieces must match exactly in overall length from tenon shoulder to shoulder. This helps ensure that the case comes together squarely and cleanly, with no gaps.

It's also crucial to locate all of the tenons correctly on the thickness of the stock so that the outside case surfaces are flush with the posts when the joint is assembled. To do this

Mortise for the runners and kickers. The top rail is dovetailed into the tops of the leg posts. The author rabbets the tail to enhance accuracy when transferring the layout.

Locate the kickers and runners. They are tenoned into the front rails and apron, and those mortises can be cut by machine, but the back panel's width means its mortises must be cut by hand. The mortise locations are picked up from the dry-fit front assembly (above) and marked on both faces of the back panel. Use a ¼-in. chisel to chop the through-mortises, working in from each surface (right).

consistently, scribe the end grain for both cheeks using the outside face as a reference for your marking gauge. Set the gauge for ¼ in. to scribe the outside cheeks and ½ in. to scribe the inside cheeks.

To cut the cheeks, set the stock face-side down on the tablesaw and raise a dado cutter to just under the lower scribe line on the end of the first workpiece. Adjust the rip fence for ¹⁄₃₂ in. less than the tenon's length and use the miter gauge to help control the workpieces. For the intermediate front rail, use a ½-in. dado stack to remove the waste from between the twin tenons. Hold the piece vertically against a miter gauge. Use a sacrificial backer block and use the miter fence as a stop. Raise the blade to just below the scribe line before making the cut.

At the workbench, use a shoulder plane to fit the tenons to their mortises. To help keep the outer surfaces flush, avoid paring too much stock from either tenon cheek. After paring to the shoulder lines with a chisel, cut the multiple tenons from the full-length tongues on the back and side panels.

Before you can start gluing up, you'll need to dovetail the top rail, then mortise the front rails and the case back for the kickers and runners that will support the drawers. Then, with the case dry-fit, locate and fit

Measure to locate the drawer partitions. The whole case is dry-fit at this point (above). The vertical drawer partitions are dovetailed into the top of the apron and the bottom of the intermediate rail. The clamp helps hold the partitions in place while you knife the profile on the front surfaces of the apron and rail (left). Now disassemble the case, saw the mortise, and chop and pare to fit.

Glue up the front and back.
Apply yellow glue to both mortises and tenons. Once each assembly is in clamps, lay a straightedge across both post blocks to make sure they don't twist out of square. On the front assembly, check the diagonal dimensions and adjust the clamps to bring it into square. Glue the partitions in place after the front assembly has dried.

the dovetailed vertical partitions. Finally, bandsaw out the shape of the front apron and clean up the profile.

Transition blocks marry legs to case

Start building the case by gluing up the back and front assemblies separately. The legs transition into the case with blocks that are glued on and shaped to match the curved profile. It's much easier to apply and shape the two blocks on the front apron now than when the case is fully glued up.

Begin by holding each block in position to see whether it is flat against the apron and the back of the knee. If needed, plane the

block to fit. When this is done, draw the pattern on the front and saw the front profile, saving the offcut. Now return to the bench, hold the block in position again, and trace the shape of the leg onto the surface of the block that mates to the leg. To bandsaw this profile, set the transition block back onto the offcut and saw, staying 1/16 in. from the line.

Glue the two front transition blocks in place using a rub joint and hold them with a spring clamp if needed. Use a chisel, rasp, and scraper to shape the blocks. The side transition blocks are attached and shaped in the same way, but are installed after the case has been glued up.

Add the transition blocks.
The blocks are shaped in place. After cutting the basic curves in the bottom and front of the block, glue it in place with a rub joint (above left). With the block in place, pare away excess material to reach the final, rounded shape. Start with a chisel, making a series of side-to-side passes (above right). Then use a carving gouge with a shallow profile in a series of bottom-to-top passes to blend the curve further (left).

The final glue-up. Back and front assemblies are joined by gluing the side panels into the rear posts, gluing the interior kickers and runners into their mortises in the front, and then settling the front assembly into position.

Wedge the tenons. The center runners are secured in back with wedged through-tenons. Glue the wedges and tap them home. When dry, saw them off and plane them flush.

Dry-fit the case for layout

The next step is to add the sides without glue and clamp the case snug so you can accurately fit the crossmembers that span the interior. These are the runners that support the drawers from underneath and the kickers that sit above the drawers and prevent them from tipping downward when pulled out. In the space separating the upper and lower drawers, the crossmembers serve both of these functions. Rip all of the runners and kickers and crosscut them to a little over final length.

Measure from the back side of the apron and middle rail to the inside of the back. Use a knife to mark these distances on the parts. Cut the tenons with a dado blade and fit

them. On the center runners and kickers, make handsaw cuts ¼ in. from the edge and ¼ in. from the shoulder to accept wedges for the through-tenons in the back panel. The left and right runners and kickers are notched to fit around the post blocks.

20 mortises, 20 tenons, one glue-up

The case is ready to come together. With clamps ready, apply glue to the mortises in the back legs and to the corresponding tenons on the sides. Seat the sides. Next, glue the center runners and kickers into their mortises in front, then apply glue to the front leg mortises and matching side tenons. Gently lower the front into place, taking care to seat the unglued tenons of the runners and kickers in the rear-panel mortises. Stand the assembly upright and use bar clamps to seat the joints. Before the glue sets, check the diagonals for square. When all is square, drive the wedges into the through-tenons at the back of the case. Clamp the side runners in place, drill into them through the back, and drive wooden pegs to secure them.

Drop finials adorn the front apron

In order to create a 1-in.-sq. platform for each drop finial and collar, glue ¼-in.-thick backer blocks to the rear of the ¾-in.-thick front apron, matching the latter's profile. Drill a ½-in.-dia. hole into the center of each platform and into two blanks for the collars. Turn and sand the finials, including the ½-in.-dia. tenon.

To mark the size of the collar, slip it over the finial's tenon and insert the tenon into the apron. Using a ³⁄₃₂-in.-thick spacer held against each edge of the platform, scribe a line around all four sides of the collar. Hand-saw to these lines and then clean up the edges with a block plane. To create the bead, bevel all eight edges, moving the piece across the bottom of a plane, then refine the curve with sandpaper. Last, glue the collar to the platform and the finial into the apron.

Crowning touch: a hand-shaped top

The two-board top has a thumb-molding profile that is characteristic for this period, and I enjoy creating it with hand tools. The top is fastened with screws through the front rail, the two top kickers, and the cleat on the top inside surface of the back panel. Elongate the screw holes in the back to accommodate movement.

Hand-Shaped Edge Profile

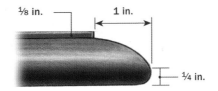

⅛ in.   1 in.   ¼ in.

No router in sight. Start by using a dado blade to cut a ⅛-in.-deep rabbet. Then use a handplane to shape the profile (left). A shoulder plane allows you to work all the way into the corner (below).

Stain and shellac for a flattering finish

I finished the piece with a water-based stain (Cuban mahogany from www. wdlockwood. com) and shellac. This approach evens out variations in the color, shows the figure well, and yields a richer tone than the brassy color that natural mahogany sometimes has. Next, I applied dark grain filler to help show the pore structure and followed with a few more coats of shellac. The last step is to rub out the finish with 0000 steel wool and apply a coat of paste wax.

Arts and Crafts on Display

MICHAEL PEKOVICH

S imple is not always easy. Take Arts and Crafts furniture. Woodworkers fond of the style—with its beefy parts, rectilinear lines, and exposed mortise-and-tenon joinery—may think the furniture is easy to make. But this simple form is unforgiving of mistakes. Make one slip-up in proportions, hardware choice, or finish, and the design falls down. I've been building Arts and Crafts furniture for a long time, and I've worked through the challenges in making a piece that's true to the style.

This case piece is an original design, yet it would not be out of place in an antique

Full-Size Template Simplifies the Sides

To cut matching mortises that align perfectly, make a full-size template from ¼-in.-thick medium-density fiberboard (MDF). The template is quick to make using a ⅜-in. straight bit on the router table.

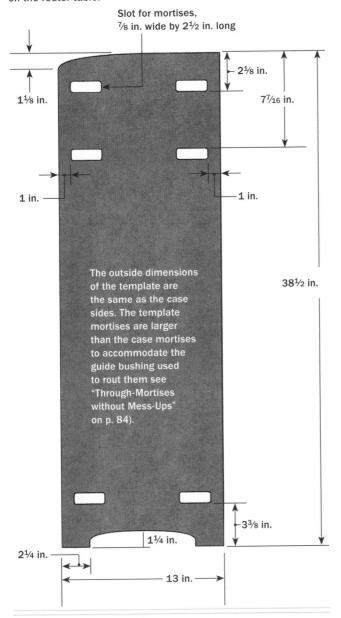

Slot for mortises,
⅞ in. wide by 2½ in. long

2⅛ in.

1⅛ in.

7⁷⁄₁₆ in.

1 in.

1 in.

The outside dimensions of the template are the same as the case sides. The template mortises are larger than the case mortises to accommodate the guide bushing used to rout them see "Through-Mortises without Mess-Ups" on p. 84).

38½ in.

3⅜ in.

1¼ in.

2¼ in.

13 in.

First cuts. Clamp stop blocks on both sides of the bit for the stopped cuts. With the spacer in place (see the drawing below), plunge through the template and make one pass in the first mortise slot. Just flip the template to do the opposite slot.

Stop Blocks and a Spacer Ensure an Accurate Template

Fence-to-bit distance: Top mortises, 2⅝ in.; divider mortises, 7¹⁵⁄₁₆ in.; bottom mortises, 3⅞ in.

1. Drop the template onto the bit and make the first pass.

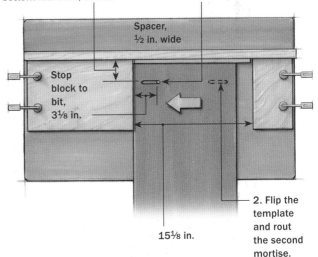

Spacer, ½ in. wide

Stop block to bit, 3⅛ in.

2. Flip the template and rout the second mortise.

15⅛ in.

Second cuts. After the first passes, remove the spacer between the fence and template and finish routing the mortise slots. Adjust the fence and repeat the process for each set of mortise slots.

Stickley catalog. With its quartersawn white oak, exposed joinery, fumed finish, and hand-hammered hardware, it breathes Arts and Crafts. The leaded-glass doors are typical too and add to the handcrafted look. You can have panels made by a local artist or you

Original Piece, Traditional Design

In Arts and Crafts furniture, it's all about the wood and small details. The tight grain and magnificent ray fleck of quartersawn oak is the primary ornamentation. To give the piece a solid feel without being clunky, the author varied the thickness of the parts. The sides are a full 1 in. thick, the top and bottom are ⅞ in. thick, and the remaining interior dividers are ¾ in. thick. Also, each piece is slightly inset from the other, creating subtle shadow lines.

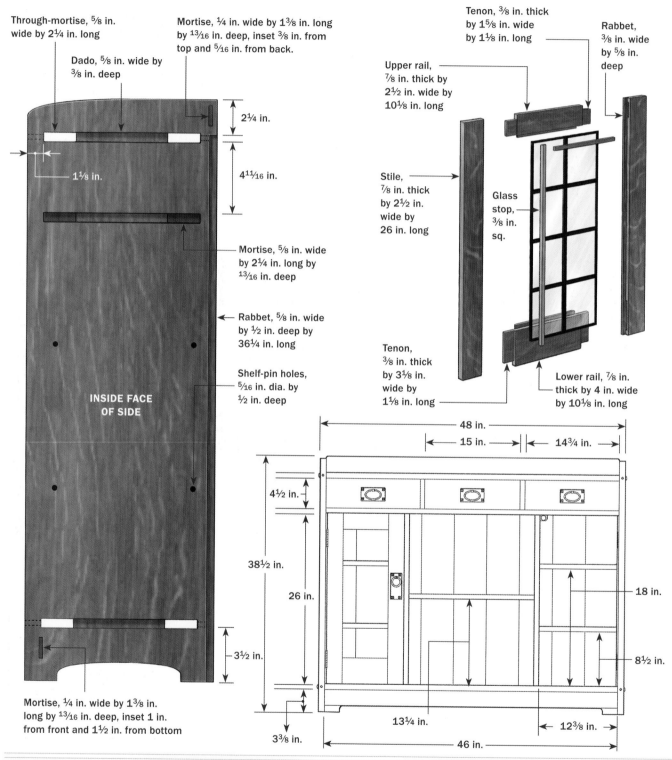

Through-mortise, ⅝ in. wide by 2¼ in. long

Dado, ⅝ in. wide by ⅜ in. deep

Mortise, ¼ in. wide by 1⅜ in. long by ¹³⁄₁₆ in. deep, inset ⅜ in. from top and ⁵⁄₁₆ in. from back.

2¼ in.

1⅛ in.

4¹¹⁄₁₆ in.

Mortise, ⅝ in. wide by 2¼ in. long by ¹³⁄₁₆ in. deep

Rabbet, ⅝ in. wide by ½ in. deep by 36¼ in. long

Shelf-pin holes, ⁵⁄₁₆ in. dia. by ½ in. deep

INSIDE FACE OF SIDE

Mortise, ¼ in. wide by 1⅜ in. long by ¹³⁄₁₆ in. deep, inset 1 in. from front and 1½ in. from bottom

Tenon, ⅜ in. thick by 1⅝ in. wide by 1⅛ in. long

Rabbet, ⅜ in. wide by ⅝ in. deep

Upper rail, ⅞ in. thick by 2½ in. wide by 10⅛ in. long

Stile, ⅞ in. thick by 2½ in. wide by 26 in. long

Glass stop, ⅜ in. sq.

Tenon, ⅜ in. thick by 3⅛ in. wide by 1⅛ in. long

Lower rail, ⅞ in. thick by 4 in. wide by 10⅛ in. long

48 in.

15 in.

14¾ in.

4½ in.

38½ in.

26 in.

18 in.

8½ in.

13¼ in.

12⅜ in.

3⅜ in.

46 in.

3½ in.

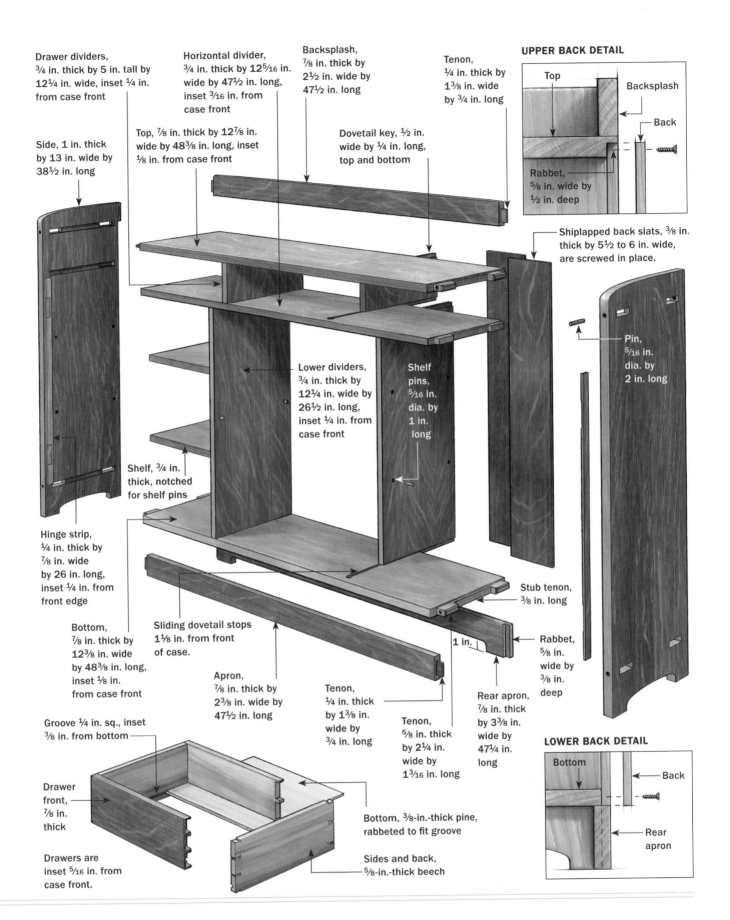

Drawer dividers, ¾ in. thick by 5 in. tall by 12¼ in. wide, inset ¼ in. from case front

Side, 1 in. thick by 13 in. wide by 38½ in. long

Horizontal divider, ¾ in. thick by 12⁵⁄₁₆ in. wide by 47½ in. long, inset ³⁄₁₆ in. from case front

Top, ⅞ in. thick by 12⅞ in. wide by 48⅜ in. long, inset ⅛ in. from case front

Backsplash, ⅞ in. thick by 2½ in. wide by 47½ in. long

Tenon, ¼ in. thick by 1⅜ in. wide by ¾ in. long

Dovetail key, ½ in. wide by ¼ in. long, top and bottom

UPPER BACK DETAIL

Top

Backsplash

Back

Rabbet, ⅝ in. wide by ½ in. deep

Shiplapped back slats, ⅜ in. thick by 5½ to 6 in. wide, are screwed in place.

Pin, ⁵⁄₁₆ in. dia. by 2 in. long

Lower dividers, ¾ in. thick by 12¼ in. wide by 26½ in. long, inset ¼ in. from case front

Shelf pins, ⁵⁄₁₆ in. dia. by 1 in. long

Shelf, ¾ in. thick, notched for shelf pins

Hinge strip, ¼ in. thick by ⅞ in. wide by 26 in. long, inset ¼ in. from front edge

Bottom, ⅞ in. thick by 12⅜ in. wide by 48⅜ in. long, inset ⅛ in. from case front

Sliding dovetail stops 1⅛ in. from front of case.

Stub tenon, ⅜ in. long

Rabbet, ⅝ in. wide by ⅜ in. deep

1 in.

Rear apron, ⅞ in. thick by 3⅜ in. wide by 47¼ in. long

Apron, ⅞ in. thick by 2⅜ in. wide by 47½ in. long

Tenon, ¼ in. thick by 1⅜ in. wide by ¾ in. long

Tenon, ⅝ in. thick by 2¼ in. wide by 1³⁄₁₆ in. long

Groove ¼ in. sq., inset ⅜ in. from bottom

Drawer front, ⅞ in. thick

Drawers are inset ⁵⁄₁₆ in. from case front.

Bottom, ⅜-in.-thick pine, rabbeted to fit groove

Sides and back, ⅝-in.-thick beech

LOWER BACK DETAIL

Bottom

Back

Rear apron

Through-Mortises without Mess-Ups

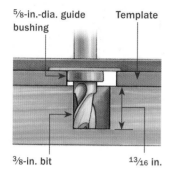

⁵⁄₈-in.-dia. guide bushing   Template

³⁄₈-in. bit   ¹³⁄₁₆ in.

Start on the inside face.
To make it easier to hold the workpiece and template, the author uses an elevated clamping table. A bushing guides a spiral upcut bit.

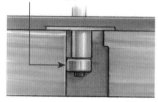

½-in. bearing-guided bit

The Paolini trick. To complete the through-mortises with no tearout, the author uses a trick he learned from Greg Paolini. Drill a hole through each mortise (right), flip over the piece, insert a bearing-guided bit in the hole, and rout out the remaining waste (far right).

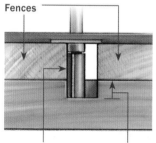

Fences

½-in. bearing-guided bit   ³⁄₈ in.

Connect the slots.
To rout the shallow dadoes that connect the through-mortises, clamp fences on both sides of the mortises and use a top-bearing-guided bit.

TIP Place tape over the divider mortises so you don't drill through them accidentally.

Two-part tenons. The dado blade does most of the work. After cutting the tenon cheeks and shoulders with a dado set, cut the through-tenons to width, using a tall fence to support the board. The scrapwood behind the tenons backs up the cut and reduces tearout.

Saw off the stub tenon. Use the bandsaw to cut the stub tenons to length. The fence ensures a parallel cut.

can make them yourself. If you are interested in building in this style, I hope you'll find a few valuable lessons here. Also, this piece is a versatile one: I designed it to hold books and cherished items, but it could work as a sideboard, too.

When building an Arts and Crafts piece, the most important step is to choose good wood. The tight grain and magnificent ray fleck of quartersawn oak is the primary ornamentation, so don't skimp on the lumber. I found some great boards online that I supplemented with lumber from a local yard.

With a large project like this, I start from the outside and work my way in because it's easier to build the case first and fit the interior dividers after. The top and bottom of the case attach to the sides with through-tenons. To help keep the case square and the wide boards flat, I added a stub tenon between the through-tenons.

The through-tenons are prominent features of the design, so you must get them right. For clean cuts and no gaps, I fitted the router with a guide bushing and straight bit and cut the mortises using a full-size template (see "Through-Mortises without Mess-Ups" and photos on the facing page). Then I cut the dadoes between mortises for the stub tenons. Finally, I squared up the mortises with a chisel.

To cut the remaining mortises for the backsplash and the lower apron, attach a fence to the router and use a spiral upcut bit. Then square them with a chisel.

Once the mortises have been cut, cut out the foot recess and profile the tops of the sides. Clean up the cuts with a block plane, a spokeshave, and files. The last task is to drill holes for the tenon pins. For this, I used a doweling jig to help keep the bit aligned.

Use a fence to guide the slot cuts. To ensure that the dovetail slots are parallel, clamp a medium-density fiberboard (MDF) fence to the workpiece to steer the router's guide bushing.

Sliding Dovetails Made Easy

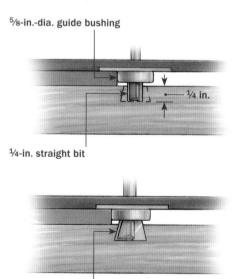

⅝-in.-dia. guide bushing

¼-in. straight bit

¼ in.

½-in. dia. 14° dovetail bit

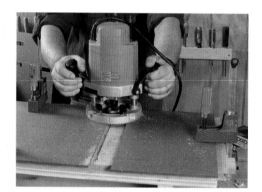

Remove the waste. Drill a ½-in.-dia. hole at the stopped end, then rough out the slot using a ¼-in. straight bit. The ¼-in. piece of MDF opposite the fence prevents the router from tipping.

Final cut. Use a ½-in. dovetail bit to finish the slot. The hole at the end of the slot lets you drop the bit into the cut before turning on the router. The hole will be hidden by the divider.

Glue-up without screw-ups. The case glue-up involves eight pieces. That many solid parts can be a pain to assemble and align during a single glue-up. So assemble the piece in stages. Start with the backsplash and apron first. Dry-fit the case to ensure proper alignment when gluing the backsplash and apron to the case top and bottom. These parts will help keep the case square in the later stages.

Top, bottom, and sides. Use grooved clamping cauls over the through-tenons to get pressure where it's needed (far left). Place the case on T-supports to make clamping easier (left). Be sure to keep glue off the ends of the through-tenons.

Crosspieces must line up shoulder to shoulder

Now it's time to cut the tenons on the top, the bottom, the horizontal divider, the backsplash, and the apron. These parts have three different tenon lengths among them, but they all have the same shoulder-to-shoulder length. To ensure the case remains square, it is critical to get this dimension exactly right.

To help, I use a trick I learned from contributing *Fine Woodworking* editor Steve Latta. Cut the parts all the same length, and then cut the tenon shoulders using the same setting on the tablesaw. Test the fit, and then trim the through-tenons to width. Next, cut

the stub tenons to length using a bandsaw. Once you're sure everything is fitting well, trim the through-tenons to their final length and chamfer their ends.

Now rout the slots for the stopped sliding dovetails that connect the vertical dividers to the top, the bottom, and the horizontal divider. Then cut the rabbets in the sides and top for the back panel.

Assembly: keep it square

It's critical that the case remains square as you assemble it. Otherwise, you'll be fighting to fit the doors and drawers. To simplify the glue-up and to help keep the case square, I first glued the backsplash and apron to the

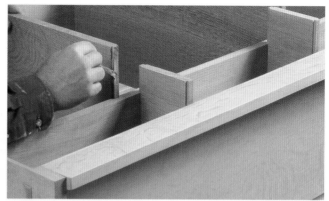

Long sliding dovetails with no binding. The trick is to slide in the dividers from the back almost all the way without glue, leaving about 2 in. exposed, and then apply glue to that exposed end and into the slot at the front. Now you can drive the divider home with a mallet.

Build the drawers and doors

With the case glued up, it's time to build and fit the drawers and doors. All three drawer fronts are cut from one board for continuous grain and color. Original Stickley pieces typically use white oak for the drawer sides as well, but I chose beech because of its dense, fine grain.

The doors are rabbeted for simple leaded-glass panels. I wanted them to be inset $5/16$ in. from the front of the case, which means I couldn't hinge them directly to the case sides. So I added ¼-in.-thick hinge strips to the inside of the case, inset ¼ in. from the front edge. The strips provide clearance for the doors to open and it's easy to cut the hinge mortises before installing them.

Vertical dividers. After cutting the dividers to length, use the dovetail bit to cut the keys. A tall fence supports the long boards and a featherboard keeps the piece snug against the fence.

case top and bottom, respectively. Then I glued up the sides, top, and bottom.

After the glue is dry, drill holes though the tenons and dry-fit the pins. Cut the pins to length and chamfer the exposed end of the pins before gluing them in.

Once the case is assembled, cut the vertical dividers to length and rout the dovetail keys on the ends, using the same dovetail bit used to rout the slots. After installing the dividers, cut and fit the shiplapped back panels.

Fumed Finish Made Easy

Fuming wood involves exposing it to ammonia fumes, which react with tannins in the oak to darken its color. The longer the wood is exposed, the darker it becomes.

Most people build a complicated tent to house the workpiece and contain the ammonia fumes. But I just drape plastic sheeting over the piece. It works as well as the tent and makes it easier to take the cover off the ammonia once it's safely inside. The sheeting also makes it easy to remove sample blocks to check the finish.

Though my method is low-tech, I still treat the ammonia carefully because it's a toxic chemical that can damage your lungs, skin, and eyes. Be sure to set up the fuming area in a low-traffic, well-ventilated area. Wear goggles and gloves when you're pouring it, and be sure to wear gloves when you take the lid off the container once it's under the plastic. Also, when you remove the sheeting, it's a good idea to run a fan in the space to help ventilate the area. The good news is that the fumes dissipate quickly.

Respirator not required. Drape plastic sheeting over the piece as a tent. Then put the ammonia in a covered container and slide it under the tent. Wear gloves when you reach under the cover to remove the lid.

How to dial in the color. The effect won't be apparent until finish is applied, so it's a good idea to throw in a few sample blocks, remove them at hour intervals, and wipe on some finish to preview the final effect.

Warm it up. Fuming imparts a greenish-gray cast to the wood. The author warmed up the look with a coat of garnet shellac before applying Waterlox. He rubbed out the finish with steel wool and brown wax made from melting Kiwi brown shoe polish into paste wax using a double-boiler setup.

Details that would make Stickley proud

No matter how true you are to the Arts and Crafts ideals when you build a piece, you can kill the design if you choose the wrong hardware or mess up the finish. For this piece, I chose traditional hand-hammered hardware (the hinges were from Horton Brasses www.horton-brasses.com, part no. PB-409B) and fumed the wood before applying a topcoat. Fuming may intimidate people, but I've developed a low-tech method (for details, see "Fumed Finish Made Easy" above).

After fuming, I warm up the wood with a coat of garnet shellac. Then I switch to Waterlox®, a wipe-on tung oil varnish. The last step is to rub out the finish with steel wool and apply a dark wax. This fills the open pores of the oak and pops the rays.

Now screw on the back slats, add the glass panels to the doors, install the traditional hardware, and the piece is ready for your living room.

The Versatile Huntboard

GARRETT HACK

The huntboard is a wonderful furniture form, a relaxed country cousin to the more formal and high-style sideboard. It's essentially a tall serving table, with drawers and doors for storage of dinnerware. I've long admired the form, so for one year's annual auction of the New Hampshire Furniture Masters, I decided to design and build a cherry huntboard.

Typically, when designing furniture, my first thoughts are about form, proportion, shape, and detail. But versatility also can be an influence, especially for speculative work.

I want potential bidders to see what they need—a sideboard in this case—but I also think my work could have many lives beyond the one I design for. This piece would be at home serving as a desk or a display table in a foyer or hallway.

The focus of my design is the three central drawers, with flanking doors adding a sense of balance. The case itself is deep and tall and is engineered to withstand the weight of a collection of flatware and dinnerware. It's also designed to withstand seasonal wood movement.

Leg Tapers

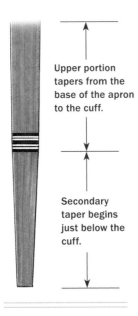

Upper portion tapers from the base of the apron to the cuff.

Secondary taper begins just below the cuff.

Start with the legs.
The foot of each leg is highlighted with a cuff-banding inlay and a secondary taper that give the piece a light, elegant appearance. After cutting the primary tapers on the bandsaw, miter and glue in the cuff-banding sections (1). Cut the secondary taper on all four sides, staying well clear of the cuff. Refine the taper with a handplane. Make guide marks just below the cuff (2) and at the toe of the foot, then plane until both marks are gone (3).

Assembly note.
The huntboard glue-up is complex. It's easiest to start by assembling the side aprons and the legs. But glue only the front legs in place at this stage—you'll need to remove the rear legs for a later step (see p. 95).

Stylish Huntboard

For a calm appearance, the primary wood is quartersawn cherry. To add interest and contrast, the door panels are flame birch, with African blackwood pulls and Gabon ebony beading.

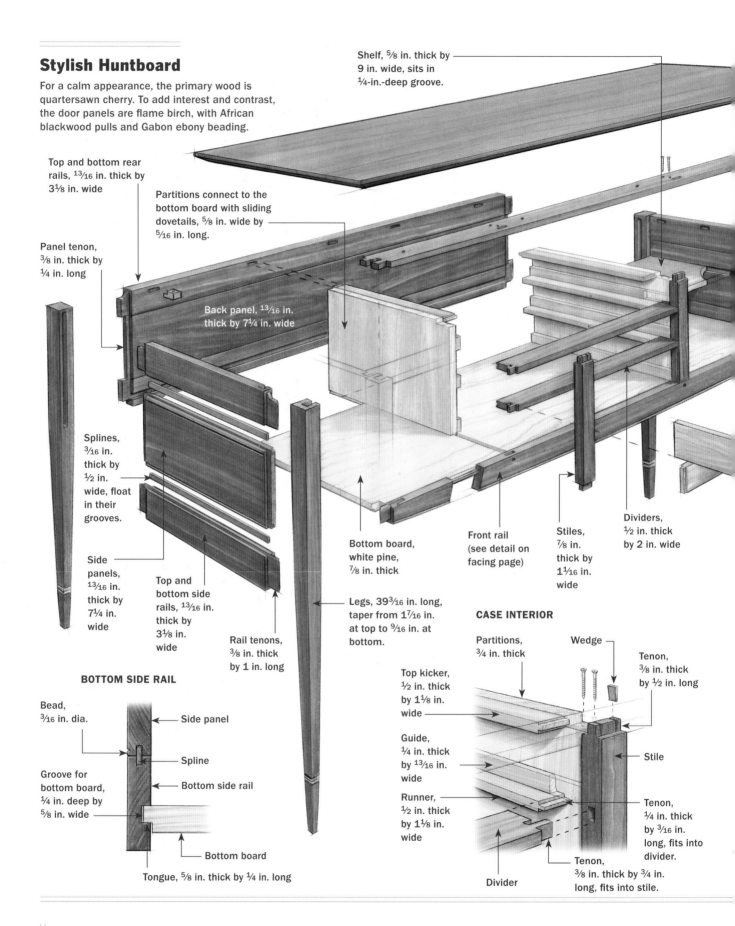

Shelf, 5/8 in. thick by 9 in. wide, sits in 1/4-in.-deep groove.

Top and bottom rear rails, 13/16 in. thick by 3 1/8 in. wide

Partitions connect to the bottom board with sliding dovetails, 5/8 in. wide by 5/16 in. long.

Panel tenon, 3/8 in. thick by 1/4 in. long

Back panel, 13/16 in. thick by 7 1/4 in. wide

Splines, 3/16 in. thick by 1/2 in. wide, float in their grooves.

Side panels, 13/16 in. thick by 7 1/4 in. wide

Top and bottom side rails, 13/16 in. thick by 3 1/8 in. wide

Rail tenons, 3/8 in. thick by 1 in. long

Bottom board, white pine, 7/8 in. thick

Front rail (see detail on facing page)

Stiles, 7/8 in. thick by 1 1/16 in. wide

Dividers, 1/2 in. thick by 2 in. wide

Legs, 39 3/16 in. long, taper from 1 7/16 in. at top to 9/16 in. at bottom.

CASE INTERIOR

Partitions, 3/4 in. thick

Wedge

Tenon, 3/8 in. thick by 1/2 in. long

Top kicker, 1/2 in. thick by 1 1/8 in. wide

Guide, 1/4 in. thick by 13/16 in. wide

Runner, 1/2 in. thick by 1 1/8 in. wide

Stile

Tenon, 1/4 in. thick by 3/16 in. long, fits into divider.

Divider

Tenon, 3/8 in. thick by 3/4 in. long, fits into stile.

BOTTOM SIDE RAIL

Bead, 3/16 in. dia.

Side panel

Spline

Groove for bottom board, 1/4 in. deep by 5/8 in. wide

Bottom side rail

Bottom board

Tongue, 5/8 in. thick by 1/4 in. long

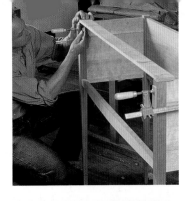

Stretcher, ½ in. thick by 2⁷⁄₁₆ in. wide by 45⅛ in. long

FRONT RAIL

Bottom board

⅛ in.

Front rail

Spline, ³⁄₁₆ in. thick by ½ in. wide

Bead, ³⁄₁₆ in. dia.

Bottom, ⁵⁄₁₆ in. thick, is beveled around the edges and screwed to the back.

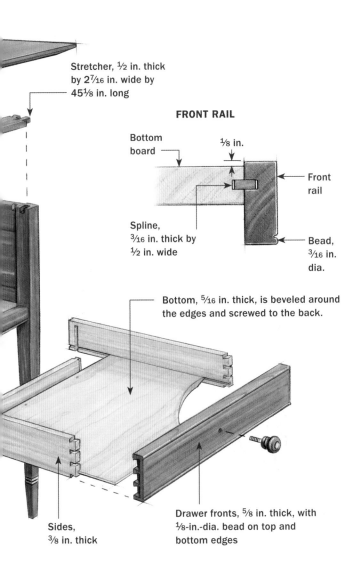

Sides, ⅜ in. thick

Drawer fronts, ⅝ in. thick, with ⅛-in.-dia. bead on top and bottom edges

Fitting a critical joint.
The front stretcher is rabbeted and dovetailed to the legs and side aprons to help stabilize the case against racking forces. Begin by marking the shoulders of the rabbet with the case dry-assembled (top). Cut the stepped rabbet using a backsaw and chisels, then saw the dovetails (middle). Set the stretcher in place and scribe for the dovetail housings in the leg and apron (bottom).

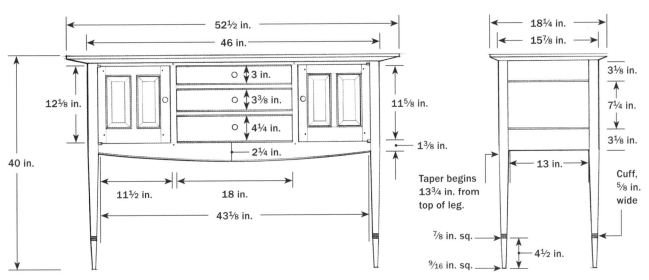

52½ in.

46 in.

18¼ in.

15⅞ in.

12⅛ in.

3 in.

3⅜ in.

4¼ in.

11⅝ in.

3⅛ in.

7¼ in.

3⅛ in.

1⅜ in.

2¼ in.

40 in.

11½ in.

18 in.

43⅛ in.

13 in.

Cuff, ⅝ in. wide

Taper begins 13¾ in. from top of leg.

⅞ in. sq.

⁹⁄₁₆ in. sq.

4½ in.

Shape the legs and add the banding

In designing the legs of the huntboard, I used a full-size mock-up to help me gauge where they needed refining. After all, visual strength is just as important as actual strength. Once I completed the mock-up, I used it to lay out and cut the real legs as well as to lay out the cuff banding and mortises. Cut the legs on the bandsaw and refine the shape with handplanes.

After cutting all of the mortises and the primary taper in the legs, install the cuff banding. Although you can make your own custom banding, ready-made banding is available (www.vandykes.com, www.wood-craft.com, and www.rockler.com). Cut the dadoes that house the banding using either a router or hand tools. Each section of banding is mitered using a 45° guide block and chisel; the block is also used to miter the door beading. After the banding is glued in place, level the sections with a block plane, then plane a tapered toe from the cuff to the floor.

Assemble the side and rear aprons

One of the most challenging aspects of this design is planning for the inevitable seasonal movement of the 13½-in.-wide aprons. Cherry boards that wide will move significantly, increasing the potential for cracking the case, opening a gap where they meet the top, and pinching a drawer or a door.

A simple and attractive solution is to make each apron in three parts: a top and bottom rail and a center panel, joined with cherry splines but no glue. The tenons of the rails are glued into the legs, while the stub tenons of the panel float in their mortises. As a decorative element, and to disguise small gaps that will open during the dry winter months, I cut beads in the center panel where it meets the rails (see "Bottom Side Rail" on p. 92).

The most accurate way to cut the tenons and shoulders on the three parts of each apron is to dry-assemble them with the splines and cut them all at once, holding the pieces together with masking tape. Clean up the shoulders with a shoulder plane, then take apart the assembly and trim the center panel tenons down to ¼ in. long. Now, cut the miters and haunches in the longer tenons of the rails. Finally, cut a groove in the bottom rail to accept the tongue of the bottom board.

Fit the front rail and stretcher

When the aprons have been fitted, it's time to cut, shape, and fit the bottom front rail. Also, cut the slot in the rail for the spline that connects it to the bottom board, and scratch the bead along the bottom edge.

The front stretcher is dovetailed into the top of the front legs and into the top of both side aprons just behind the legs (see the photos on p. 93). For accuracy, dry-assemble the case and place the rail in position. Lay out the location of the shoulders and dovetails and then cut them. Place the rail back in position, mark the dovetail housings, then rout and chop them out. Finally, cut the mortises for the two kickers of the top drawer into the back edge of the stretcher. Also, cut the mortises for the knife hinges in the stretcher and the bottom front rail.

Jig creates perfect bead stock. The jig is a piece of ½-in.-thick plywood with two fences spaced the width of a block plane. The plane rides on identical shims, ensuring uniform thickness. A brad in front of the beading holds it in place.

for the buttons that secure the top as well as the mortises in the rear apron for the two top-drawer kickers. Once you're sure everything is fitting nicely, get ready for the glue-up.

There are a lot of pieces to put together here, so to make the job easier, assemble the case in steps. After the case is glued up, cut the top to final dimensions, shape the under-beveled edge, and secure it in place with buttons and screws.

Finally, after building the doors, assembling the drawers, and turning and installing the knobs, the piece is ready for finishing.

Build doors and drawers after glue-up

When all the partitions have been cut and fitted, dry-assemble the piece, then lay out and cut the slots in the partition and side apron for the shelf that's tucked behind one door. Also, lay out and cut all the mortises

Glue the beading to the frame. The beading should be proud of the outside of the frame. Use plenty of clamps and a caul to ensure a good bond.

Simple jig for perfect miters. Clamp a 45° guide block to the frame members and chop the beading to length.

Doors Feature Contrasting Beading

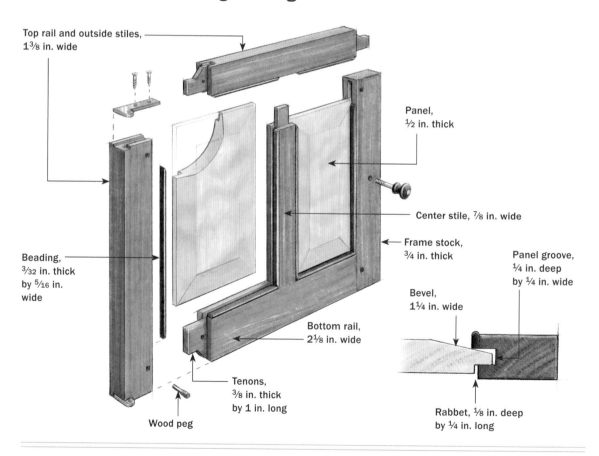

Top rail and outside stiles, 1 3/8 in. wide

Panel, 1/2 in. thick

Center stile, 7/8 in. wide

Frame stock, 3/4 in. thick

Panel groove, 1/4 in. deep by 1/4 in. wide

Beading, 3/32 in. thick by 5/16 in. wide

Bevel, 1 1/4 in. wide

Bottom rail, 2 1/8 in. wide

Tenons, 3/8 in. thick by 1 in. long

Rabbet, 1/8 in. deep by 1/4 in. long

Wood peg

Run a simple scratch stock along the beading. You're done when the cutter just starts to bite into the frame.

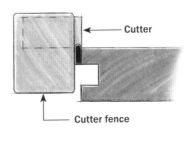

Cutter

Cutter fence

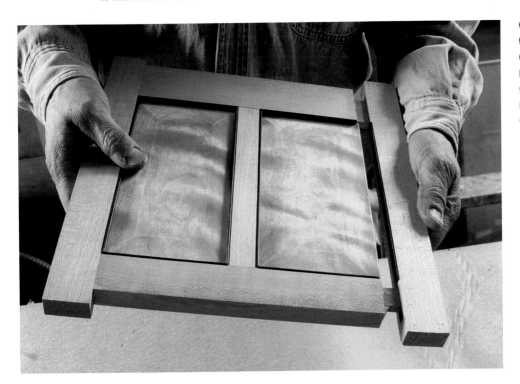

Cut the panel grooves, then assemble the door. Cutting the grooves after the beading is applied ensures a flush fit between panel and beading. Trim the horns after the glue dries.

Nothing beats the dazzle of shellac

To bring out the rich color of the cherry, I started with a light coat of oil/varnish. Once dry, I padded on many layers of orange shellac (1-lb. cut) using a clean cotton rubber, rubbing it out between coats with 0000 steel wool. A final ghosting with a rag with just vapors of alcohol leaves a beautifully smooth finish. A topcoat of wax is the final and renewable protective finish.

Sleek TV Console

ANATOLE BURKIN

I was the last man on my block, maybe in the entire country, to buy a flat-screen digital television. Like many people, I used to hide my television in an entertainment armoire, but the latest flat-screen televisions have a modern look that I find attractive. Also, it takes a pretty huge cabinet to contain them. So instead of hiding the TV, I hung it on the wall and decided to build a sleek entertainment credenza to go under it.

Made of ¾-in.-thick sapele plywood and solid sapele and wenge, the piece fits into the modernist style—with its clean, crisp lines, no exposed joinery, and no frame-and-panel doors, just long expanses of beautiful sapele grain framed by darker wenge.

Style, however, does not trump function. This credenza offers plenty of storage. Inside are three compartments hidden by three sliding doors. The center section holds the electronics: DVD player, receiver, cable box, and a laptop. The outer sections have banks of drawers to store CDs, DVDs, and other accessories, like headphones and cables. If you don't own a lot of CDs and DVDs, you could easily eliminate the drawers and use that space to hold game consoles or other electronic gear or even change the overall dimensions. The design is quite versatile.

Start with the carcase joinery

Rough-cut the plywood to manageable pieces using a circular saw and an edge guide. Make the final cuts using the tablesaw and a sled. You'll need to cut the top and bottom ½ in. longer than shown in the drawing. I did this to make the joinery simpler to cut. These two pieces will be trimmed ¼ in. on each end after cutting the mortises. Use a block plane to clean up any sawmarks on the edges.

Next, use a dado set to rabbet the back of all four carcase parts. Glue blocks on the inside corners strengthen the case and provide a stable platform when routing the mortises in the sides. Mill up the blocks and glue them flush to the top and bottom edges and ½-in. back from the front edge to allow for the face frame.

Cut mortises for the slip tenons

A fence-equipped router works fine to cut the mortises for this project, but I splurged last year and bought a Festool® Domino® joiner, which makes really fast work of mortise-and-tenon joinery. The tool cuts a deep mortise in one plunge, like a biscuit joiner. I used Domino's medium-thickness bit and tenons, set to cut as deeply as possible into the sides but just shy of blowing through the top and bottom panels.

(continued on p. 104)

Glue blocks beef up the corners. The glue blocks, attached to the top and bottom of each side, increase strength against racking.

Super-Strong Corner Joint for Plywood

Corner inlay, ¼ in. by ¼ in.

⅝ in.

Top

Domino tenon (8×40), trimmed to 1¹⁄₁₆ in. long

⁷⁄₁₆ in.

⅝ in.

½ in.

Side

Glue block, ⅝ in. thick by 2 in. wide

More tenons, more strength. Festool's Domino creates rows of slip-tenon joints in minutes. In the sides, the author moved the mortises partway into the glue blocks to accommodate the rabbet that follows.

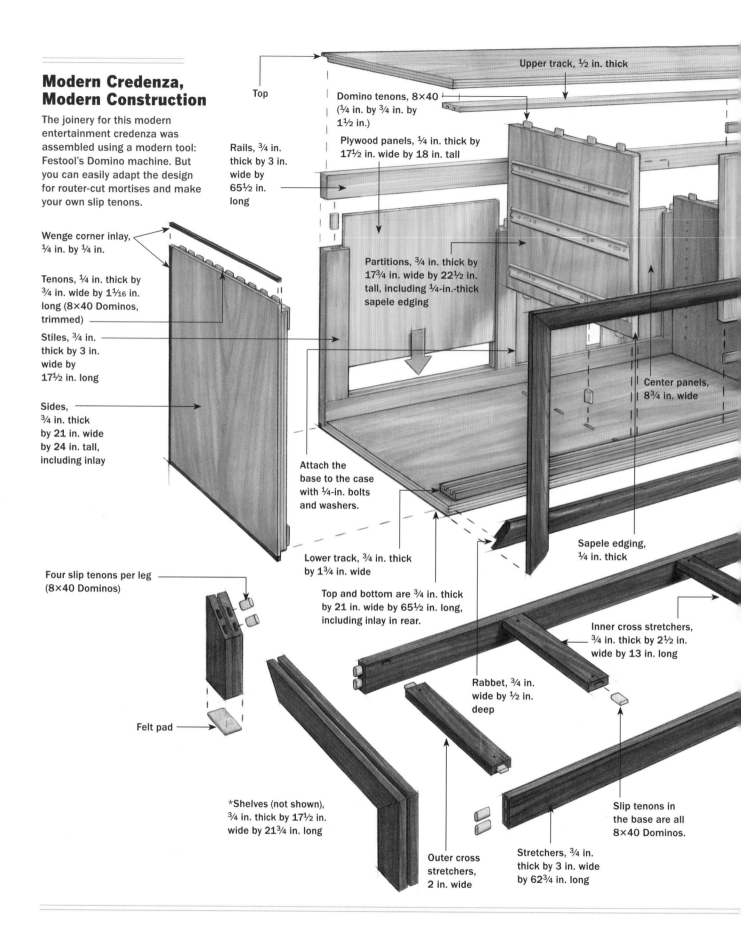

Modern Credenza, Modern Construction

The joinery for this modern entertainment credenza was assembled using a modern tool: Festool's Domino machine. But you can easily adapt the design for router-cut mortises and make your own slip tenons.

Wenge corner inlay, ¼ in. by ¼ in.

Tenons, ¼ in. thick by ¾ in. wide by 1¹⁄₁₆ in. long (8×40 Dominos, trimmed)

Stiles, ¾ in. thick by 3 in. wide by 17½ in. long

Sides, ¾ in. thick by 21 in. wide by 24 in. tall, including inlay

Top

Upper track, ½ in. thick

Domino tenons, 8×40 (¼ in. by ¾ in. by 1½ in.)

Rails, ¾ in. thick by 3 in. wide by 65½ in. long

Plywood panels, ¼ in. thick by 17½ in. wide by 18 in. tall

Partitions, ¾ in. thick by 17¾ in. wide by 22½ in. tall, including ¼-in.-thick sapele edging

Center panels, 8¾ in. wide

Attach the base to the case with ¼-in. bolts and washers.

Sapele edging, ¼ in. thick

Four slip tenons per leg (8×40 Dominos)

Lower track, ¾ in. thick by 1¾ in. wide

Top and bottom are ¾ in. thick by 21 in. wide by 65½ in. long, including inlay in rear.

Rabbet, ¾ in. wide by ½ in. deep

Inner cross stretchers, ¾ in. thick by 2½ in. wide by 13 in. long

Felt pad

Slip tenons in the base are all 8×40 Dominos.

*Shelves (not shown), ¾ in. thick by 17½ in. wide by 21¾ in. long

Outer cross stretchers, 2 in. wide

Stretchers, ¾ in. thick by 3 in. wide by 62¾ in. long

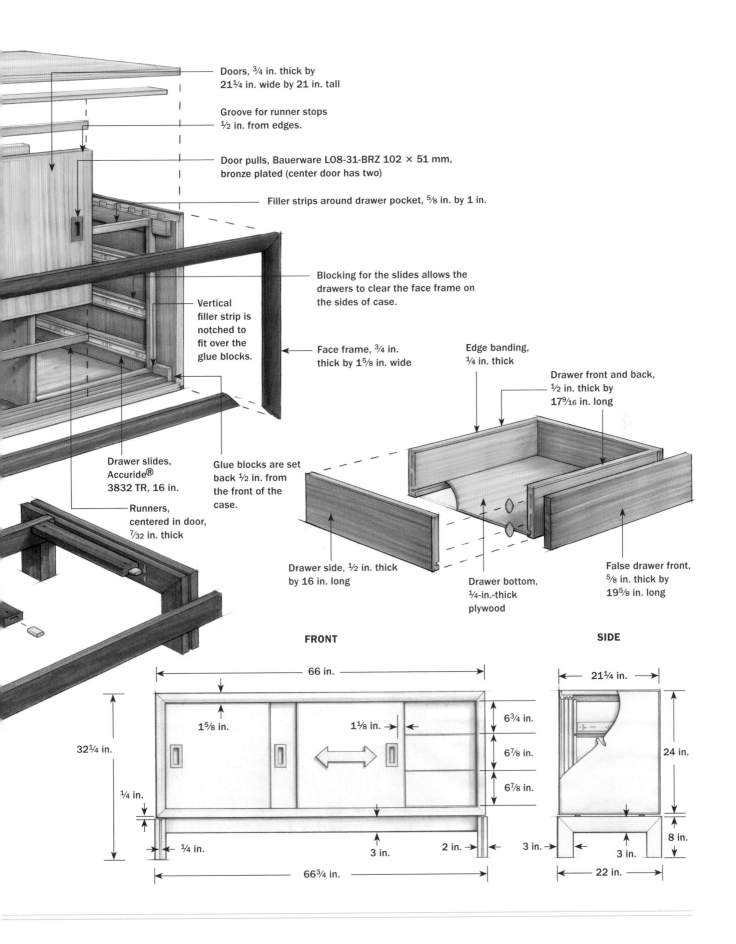

Doors, ³⁄₄ in. thick by 21¹⁄₄ in. wide by 21 in. tall

Groove for runner stops ¹⁄₂ in. from edges.

Door pulls, Bauerware LO8-31-BRZ 102 × 51 mm, bronze plated (center door has two)

Filler strips around drawer pocket, ⁵⁄₈ in. by 1 in.

Blocking for the slides allows the drawers to clear the face frame on the sides of case.

Vertical filler strip is notched to fit over the glue blocks.

Face frame, ³⁄₄ in. thick by 1⁵⁄₈ in. wide

Edge banding, ¹⁄₄ in. thick

Drawer front and back, ¹⁄₂ in. thick by 17⁹⁄₁₆ in. long

Drawer slides, Accuride® 3832 TR, 16 in.

Glue blocks are set back ¹⁄₂ in. from the front of the case.

Runners, centered in door, ⁷⁄₃₂ in. thick

Drawer side, ¹⁄₂ in. thick by 16 in. long

Drawer bottom, ¹⁄₄-in.-thick plywood

False drawer front, ⁵⁄₈ in. thick by 19⁵⁄₈ in. long

FRONT

SIDE

66 in.

1⁵⁄₈ in.

1¹⁄₈ in.

32¹⁄₄ in.

¹⁄₄ in.

¹⁄₄ in.

3 in.

2 in.

66³⁄₄ in.

6³⁄₄ in.

6⁷⁄₈ in.

6⁷⁄₈ in.

21¹⁄₄ in.

24 in.

8 in.

3 in.

3 in.

22 in.

Trim the top. After cutting the mortises in the top and bottom, trim those parts to fit inside the rabbets in the sides.

Use a dado set to rabbet the sides. Bury the blade in a sacrificial fence to dial in the width. Place an offcut from the glue-block stock under the workpiece to stabilize it.

No matter what tool you use, mark out the joinery using a story stick. Once that's done, go ahead and start cutting mortises. Use the outside faces of the carcase components as reference points for the fence of your router or Domino.

I put ¼-in. wenge inlay in each corner of this plywood case, which not only adds a nice contrast but also offers a more durable edge. The rabbet joints are designed to leave a pocket for this inlay.

Rabbet the top and bottom of the sides using a dado set, sneaking up on a good fit. You will have removed some of the mortise depth, hence the deep initial cuts. Next, trim ¼ in. off each end of the top and bottom to accommodate the rabbets.

Finally, cut the partitions to size and drill the shelf-pin holes in them for the adjustable shelves. Add the solid-wood edging on the front and cut the mortises in the partitions and the top and bottom for the slip tenons.

Dry-fit and glue up the case

When it comes to gluing up the case, a dry run is critical. It gives you a chance to rehearse the steps, check the joints, and be sure you have enough clamps at the ready. Because the rabbets effectively reduce the depth of the mortises on the sides, stock Domino tenons have to be trimmed.

Glue the tenons into the sides and partitions, then fit them to the top and bottom. Assemble the case, making sure to check for square. For the inlay along the top, bottom, and back, mill up strips of wenge just a hair over ¼ in. sq. and glue them in; I used a pin nailer instead of clamps to hold the pieces in

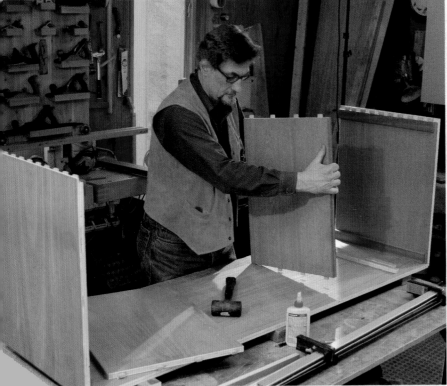

Get the glue on. Begin by gluing the slip tenons to the vertical members. Then apply glue to the mortises of the top and bottom. Clamp along the edges and use cauls to bring home the partitions.

Cut the partition joinery. To align the mortises in the top and bottom, use a spacer board to guide the Domino joiner. Reference the spacer board off the side, which should be dry-fitted in place.

Fill the rabbets. Glue and nail (or tape) the wenge inlay strips to the corners and back edges of the case. Trim them flush after the glue dries.

Glued-in panels create a rigid assembly. A sturdy back helps strengthen the case against racking. The two outer panels are glued into their grooves; the two center panels (not shown) are removable. The frame is connected with slip tenons and screwed into the cabinet.

Mitered Wenge Frame for the Front

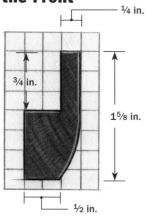

¼ in.

¾ in.

1⅝ in.

½ in.

Roundover on the router table. Rout the profile on the stock before cutting the miters. Fair the shape with handplanes, scrapers, and sandpaper.

Sled makes better miters. After rabbeting the back of the stock, cut the miters using a sled. Place a scrap piece in the rabbet to support the workpiece.

place. The pins are set deep enough to be out of the way later when I plane the inlay flush.

Add the back

The back assembly is a solid-wood sapele frame with ¼-in.-thick sapele-faced medium-density fiberboard (MDF) or plywood panels. The end panels are fixed; the center panels are removable for easy access to wiring.

Plane the frame assembly to fit the carcase, then screw it in place. I didn't glue the frame, figuring that in a few years I might want to change the inside of the case to accommodate new technology.

Attach the front face frame

A solid wenge face frame that is mitered and rabbeted to fit over the plywood, decorates

Glue the frame to the front. Rather than fussing with clamps, the author used pins to hold the pieces in place. Pieces are cut, fit, and nailed one at a time.

the front of the case. I also shaped the front face with a massive roundover bit ($2^{19}/_{32}$ in., Freud® No. 99-027) to soften the look of this otherwise squarish credenza.

Mill up the frame pieces, rabbet them, miter the corners, then glue them in place. Again, a pin nailer comes in handy.

Tackle the doors, drawers, and shelves

The sliding doors are ¾-in. plywood edged with solid sapele. Cut the plywood to size and apply the edging. The corners of the doors will be mostly hidden, so don't bother mitering the edging. Cut stopped grooves in the top and bottom edges using a slot-cutting bit in a router table. Insert runners or guides of resawn solid sapele, but don't glue them yet.

Make the tracks from solid stock. Note that the top track is thinner than the lower track. Cut the grooves on the tablesaw, mak-

Smooth Sliding Door

Upper track,
½ in. thick by 1¾ in. wide

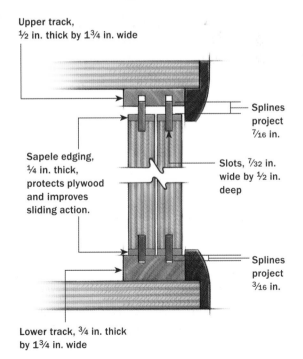

Splines project ⁷/₁₆ in.

Sapele edging, ¼ in. thick, protects plywood and improves sliding action.

Slots, ⁷/₃₂ in. wide by ½ in. deep

Splines project ³/₁₆ in.

Lower track, ¾ in. thick by 1¾ in. wide

Make tracks. The top track is thinner than the lower track. After cutting the grooves on the tablesaw, screw the tracks inside the case.

Install the runners. Rout stopped grooves in the top and bottom of the doors. Dry-fit the runners, then check the fit and action of the doors. You may have to adjust the height of the runners to get them to fit nicely.

Lift and drop. The doors are inserted from the front by tipping them into the center bay (without shelves in place). Lift the door to engage the top track first, then drop it into the lower track.

ing them a hair wider than the guides for smooth operation. Screw the tracks in place.

The doors are inserted from the front by tipping them into the center bay (without shelves in place), then lifting them to engage the top track first, and dropping them into the lower track. You may have to adjust the height of the splines to get the doors to fit.

There should be a slight gap, 1/16 in. or so, between the front and the rear door, as well as the face frame. Once you have the doors fitted to your liking, glue the guides into the doors.

I used bronze-finished metal pulls because I like a bit of metal on a modern piece. After excavating the mortises for the pulls, I used epoxy to bond the metal to the wood.

To continue the clean look inside, the drawers have no pulls. Instead, I chose full-extension touch-release slides that pop out the drawer when you push on the front. The

Tenons brace the corners. Each miter gets four slip tenons (left). Glue up the mitered feet first (above). Then attach them to the stretcher assembly (below left).

Bolt the base to the case. Drill clearance holes through the base and bottom of the case, then bolt the assembly in place.

slides provide smooth action and full access to the drawer. The drawers are ½-in. sapele plywood edged with solid sapele, with solid sapele false fronts. Shelves are ¾-in.-thick sapele plywood edged with solid wenge on the front.

Solid-wood base can handle the load

The case sits on solid wenge legs joined with stretchers, all laminated for extra thickness (I could find only 4/4 stock). The legs are slightly proud of the case on the front, sides, and rear, and the stretchers are inset to give the illusion that the case is floating. To add a shadow line, the center lamination is ¼ in. narrower than the outside pieces. It is glued

flush to one side, and indented ¼ in. on the show face. Plane and sand the show edge before glue-up, because it won't be easy to do later.

Building the base is straightforward. The corners are mitered and joined with quadruple slip tenons. A pair of stretchers ¼-in. proud of the top of the legs join the leg assemblies. Four short cross-stretchers provide support and attachment points for the case.

For the finish, a Danish Modern look goes well, nothing too glossy or grain filling. Good choices are wipe-on finishes such as Minwax poly or Waterlox. Wax the door bottoms and guides for smooth action.

A Low Console for Home Theater

STEVE CASEY

J ust a few years ago, building an entertainment center for a large-screen TV meant designing a case piece big enough to hide an elephant. Today's slimmer sets can hang on a wall or sit attractively in the open, offering furniture makers new options. Among the most practical is a low console that can house media and electronics. It's a great way to bring that glorious high-definition picture out of the armoire.

I designed this console for a self-contained small home-theater system built around a 52-in. projection-style TV, but it would work just as well with a slimmer flat-panel model. Visually, it's tasteful and tame enough to har-

Open Shelving

The components are accessible to hands and remote controls and become part of the design. The center shelving adjusts to fit a wide variety of components.

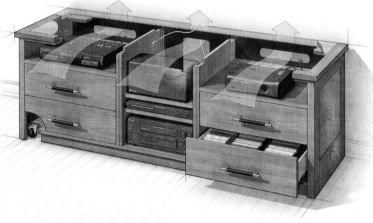

Tall drawers. Side-mounted slides allow deep storage for DVDs and CDs. Dividers keep everything organized.

A back that breathes. Multiple cutouts provide ample airflow for electronic components. The recessed back also creates space behind the piece for cords to drop freely.

Hidden wheels. Six casters make it easy to reach the back for setup, maintenance, or cleaning. The wheels are inset to avoid a distracting gap between the floor and the bottom of the piece.

monize with quite a few furniture styles, and you can feel free to adapt its style to fit your room. Look below the surface, though, and it becomes clear this piece is media furniture through and through.

At 24 in. tall, the console is still low enough to place the center of most TVs at eye level for a seated viewer. And it's strong enough to support any set, so you won't need a tricky wall-mount.

At 22 in. deep, the cabinet will comfortably hold most electronic components. I designed the drawers specifically to house DVDs and CDs without making the case too tall. The back and shelves are engineered to promote ventilation for the equipment

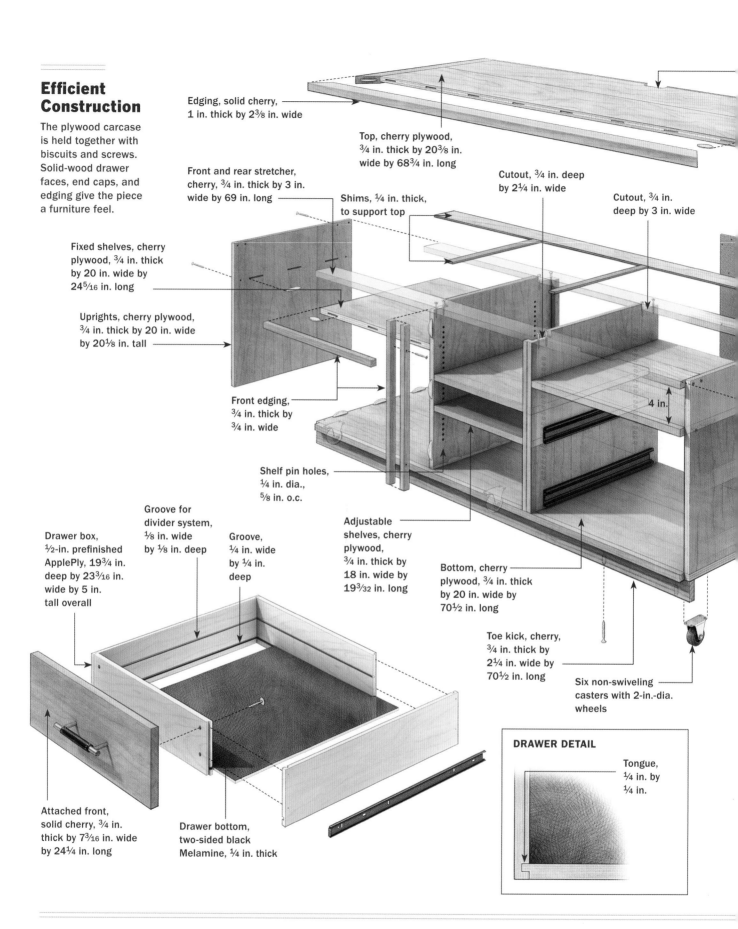

Efficient Construction

The plywood carcase is held together with biscuits and screws. Solid-wood drawer faces, end caps, and edging give the piece a furniture feel.

Edging, solid cherry, 1 in. thick by 2⅜ in. wide

Top, cherry plywood, ¾ in. thick by 20⅜ in. wide by 68¾ in. long

Cutout, ¾ in. deep by 2¼ in. wide

Cutout, ¾ in. deep by 3 in. wide

Front and rear stretcher, cherry, ¾ in. thick by 3 in. wide by 69 in. long

Shims, ¼ in. thick, to support top

Fixed shelves, cherry plywood, ¾ in. thick by 20 in. wide by 24⁵⁄₁₆ in. long

Uprights, cherry plywood, ¾ in. thick by 20 in. wide by 20⅛ in. tall

Front edging, ¾ in. thick by ¾ in. wide

4 in.

Shelf pin holes, ¼ in. dia., ⅝ in. o.c.

Groove for divider system, ⅛ in. wide by ⅛ in. deep

Groove, ¼ in. wide by ¼ in. deep

Drawer box, ½-in. prefinished ApplePly, 19¾ in. deep by 23³⁄₁₆ in. wide by 5 in. tall overall

Adjustable shelves, cherry plywood, ¾ in. thick by 18 in. wide by 19³⁄₃₂ in. long

Bottom, cherry plywood, ¾ in. thick by 20 in. wide by 70½ in. long

Toe kick, cherry, ¾ in. thick by 2¼ in. wide by 70½ in. long

Six non-swiveling casters with 2-in.-dia. wheels

Attached front, solid cherry, ¾ in. thick by 7³⁄₁₆ in. wide by 24¼ in. long

Drawer bottom, two-sided black Melamine, ¼ in. thick

DRAWER DETAIL

Tongue, ¼ in. by ¼ in.

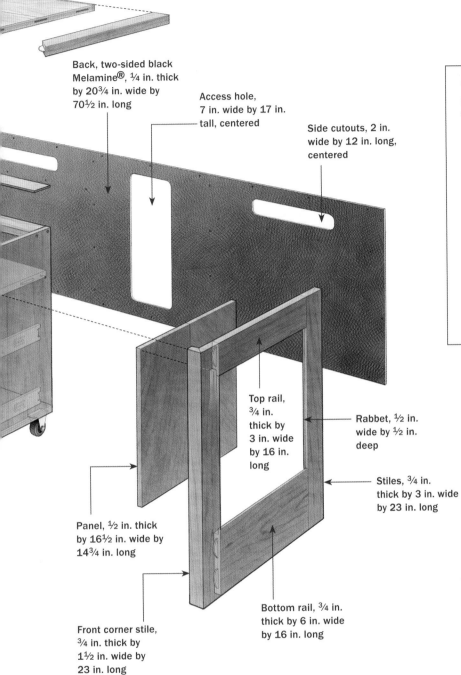

Cutout for TV cables,
7/8 in. deep by 4 in. wide

Back, two-sided black
Melamine®, 1/4 in. thick
by 20 3/4 in. wide by
70 1/2 in. long

Access hole,
7 in. wide by 17 in.
tall, centered

Side cutouts, 2 in.
wide by 12 in. long,
centered

Top rail,
3/4 in.
thick by
3 in. wide
by 16 in.
long

Rabbet, 1/2 in.
wide by 1/2 in.
deep

Stiles, 3/4 in.
thick by 3 in. wide
by 23 in. long

Panel, 1/2 in. thick
by 16 1/2 in. wide by
14 3/4 in. long

Front corner stile,
3/4 in. thick by
1 1/2 in. wide by
23 in. long

Bottom rail, 3/4 in.
thick by 6 in. wide
by 16 in. long

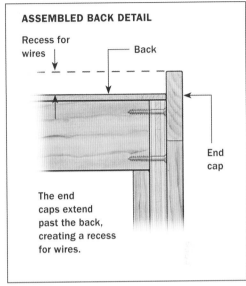

ASSEMBLED BACK DETAIL

Recess for
wires

Back

End
cap

The end
caps extend
past the back,
creating a recess
for wires.

and to simplify cable management. And I put the whole piece on casters so it would be easy to pull away from the wall for system setup, maintenance, or cleaning. Small casters will work on a hardwood floor, but carpet calls for larger ones.

None of those features calls attention to itself. What you see and live with is a nice piece of furniture. The project is a good ex-

The fixed shelves are first. Construction begins with two H-shaped subassemblies (top). These assemblies are then connected by a plywood bottom (above). The space between them creates the central shelving area.

ample of building a sturdy carcase in an efficient way, using sheet goods and techniques I developed and use for building large-scale entertainment center furniture and cabinetry.

Sheet goods make a stable case

One of the greatest challenges in building furniture to house electronic equipment is that the gear generates heat that causes wood movement. So, I always use stable composite material (in this case, two sheets of cherry plywood) for media furniture carcases.

The first step is to lay out and cut the carcase parts. When cutting sheet goods, never assume that the original edges are straight or square. If you want a 20-in.-wide finished piece, cut it at least ⅛ in. larger, then turn it around and cut off the factory edge. If things are not square, it is usually best to square the ends of smaller ripped parts rather than the whole sheet. After all the parts are cut, I drill holes for adjustable shelves in the equipment rack space. Then I join the carcase together.

The carcase is joined entirely with biscuits and screws—no dadoes, no rabbets, no glue. I don't want to chip out the veneer on a new sheet of plywood while cutting dado and rabbet joinery or fret over squeeze-out marring my finish in the corners. A glueless carcase also lets me disassemble the piece as needed during construction to check the fit and measurements, making it much easier to fix mistakes.

There's no harm, of course, in using glue if you want to. But, after years of gluing everything to last an eternity, I've discovered that biscuits and screws are more than strong enough to hold a piece like this together . . . forever.

I predrill for the screws using a tapered bit with an integral countersink. I use #7 by 1⅝-in. bugle-head construction screws with sharp, coarse threads and put them in care-

The panel sits in a rabbet. Rout the rabbet with a bearing-guided bit and square up the corners with a chisel.

A No-Clamp Glue-Up

Bevel the front stile after glue-up (1). Cutting it beforehand would deprive you of a square clamping surface. The mating piece is cut from the same stock. Strips of painters' tape align the edges and create a hinge for the glue-up (2). I wrap the assembly with several bands of painters' tape to secure the pieces (3). No biscuits or clamps are needed.

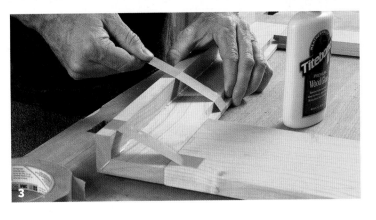

The mitered return hides the plywood. The panel is prefinished to prevent wood movement from exposing any unfinished areas at the edges.

fully so they don't strip. It's easy to get splitting near the outside joint edges, so I put a clamp on the thread side of the joint so the wedge action of the screw doesn't split the panel.

Attach the solid trim

Solid-wood edging and other details elevate the console's appearance from cabinetry to furniture. The most prominent of these features are the frame-and-panel caps on the ends. The front stiles are cut from the same stock as the side panels and are mitered to wrap the grain continuously from the sides to the face to give it the look of solid stock. The frames are assembled with biscuits and the inside of each frame is rabbeted to accept a floating panel of ½-in. solid cherry

No measuring, no marking. The lower slides sit right on the case bottom. To ensure proper spacing between the slides, the author rips a piece of ½-in. medium-density fiberboard (MDF) to match the drawer-face height.

Use the spacer to locate the upper slides. With the spacer positioned on top of the lower slide, its top edge supports the upper slide at the correct height for installation.

Solid-wood stretchers connect the piece at the top. These also create a place to attach the back and top of the cabinet. The front stretcher protrudes ¾ in. from the case to meet the other edging, so the author uses a piece of ¾-in. scrap to set the reveal.

or cherry plywood. This creates a ¼-in. reveal for the panel while maintaining consistent thickness for the exterior trim. The assembly is attached with screws driven into the frame from inside the case.

A solid-cherry stretcher across the top of the case combines with solid edging to dress out the rest of the case front. Before attaching the edging, I hand-sand a ¹⁄₁₆-in. roundover radius on the inside corners of each adjoining piece of plywood and solid stock, including the pieces on the top. This creates a very fine parting line where the plywood and edging meet, accentuating what many folks would try to hide and, in the process, making an eye-pleasing detail. After the edging is attached, I rout a ³⁄₁₆-in. roundover onto all the outside and inside corners.

The drawers have simple joinery and false fronts

I build the drawers from ½-in.-thick pre-finished AplePly® or Europlywood. The bottoms are two-sided, ¼-in. black Melamine, in keeping with the high-tech contents. The joints are rabbeted, glued, and pinned with brads to hold them together while the glue dries.

Attach the matching hardware. The author uses a combination square referenced off the bottom of the drawer side to pencil a layout line for the runner (left). Mounting screws are centered on this line and driven through factory-drilled holes in the hardware (right).

I hang the drawers on black, side-mounted, full-extension slides. Undermount slides might yield a cleaner look, but they steal depth from the drawer at the bottom. In a console with limited overall height, this can make the difference between a drawer that can be used for media storage and one that isn't deep enough.

False fronts and media storage. The author drills oversize holes and uses a 1-in. washer-head screw with a ½-in.-dia head (some manufacturers call them "drawer-front adjusting screws"). This creates wiggle room for slight adjustments in the position of the drawer front to get it square and even in the opening. The central horizontal groove houses the divider hardware.

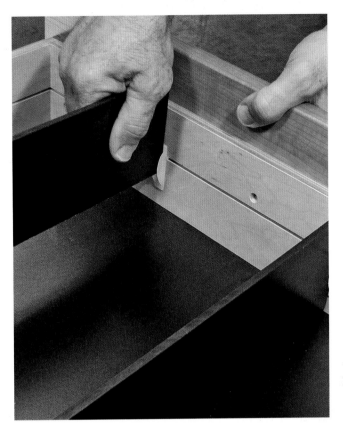

I size the drawer boxes to accommodate a ¾-in.-thick separate front, with the faces recessed very slightly behind the front radius detail. Separate drawer fronts allow for perfect alignment after the piece is finally placed and loaded with equipment.

Edge the top and attach it

The top is plywood with a 1-in. by 2½-in. solid border, which is biscuited and mitered. This three-sided border creates a nice effect, making the piece appear to belong up against a wall. The raw edge on the back of the top is dressed with ¼-in. solid stock.

To make room for the cables that connect the TV to the other equipment, make a small cutout in the back of the top. This also lets some heat escape when the case is tight against the wall. The top is held in place with screws driven from the underside through the solid cross-members of the case. Because the solid border is thicker than the top, you'll need to shim and fill the space between the plywood and the cabinet.

The back is two-sided, ¼-in. black Melamine. Although thin, this material creates a rigid back that lends the piece much of its structural strength, so be sure to size the back to fit snugly between the rear stiles of the end caps. I fasten the back with screws countersunk and driven every 8 in. into the rear edges of the plywood carcase.

Get the popcorn ready

Before finishing, break down all removable components, then sand everything that wasn't sanded before assembly. I used clear oil to bring up the color before spraying on a standard lacquer finish: one coat of sanding sealer and two coats of 40-sheen lacquer, sanding with 320-grit paper between coats. For an alternative hand-applied topcoat, try dewaxed shellac or a traditional oil finish.

Install the equipment, roll the finished unit into place, and you're all done. Time to pop in a DVD or watch some drivel on TV!

Wall Cabinet in Cherry

MATTHEW TEAGUE

Most every home has a narrow wall—usually at the end of a hallway or beside an entry door—where nothing seems to fit. This piece was designed for such a space. I keep tall vases in the cabinet and candles in the lower drawer, but it can be adapted easily to all sorts of needs. Add a few drawers, and you have a good spot for sewing supplies. With more shelves, this piece makes a handsome spice cabinet; the lower drawer is perfect for storing teas or loose spices.

Instead of using elaborate moldings, raised panels, or an arched door, this cabinet design highlights the basic joinery that is the standard in quality woodworking. Traditional dovetail joinery holds the case together, while sliding dovetails lock the shelves into place. The door is a simple frame-and-panel assembly, but I chose bridle joints instead of traditional mortises and tenons because the exposed joinery complements the through-dovetails on the case. Instead of cutting a raised or fielded panel, I opted for the clean look of a flat panel.

An efficient method for dovetailing the carcase

I cut the dovetails with a combination of traditional methods and power tools. The tails are cut first, using a ½-in. by 14° dovetail bit and a shopmade sled that is run against a fence on the router table. The first and last pins should be inset about ⅜ in.

Cherry Cabinet

The small size of this project makes it ideal for practicing dovetails and learning a quick and handsome frame-and-panel joint.

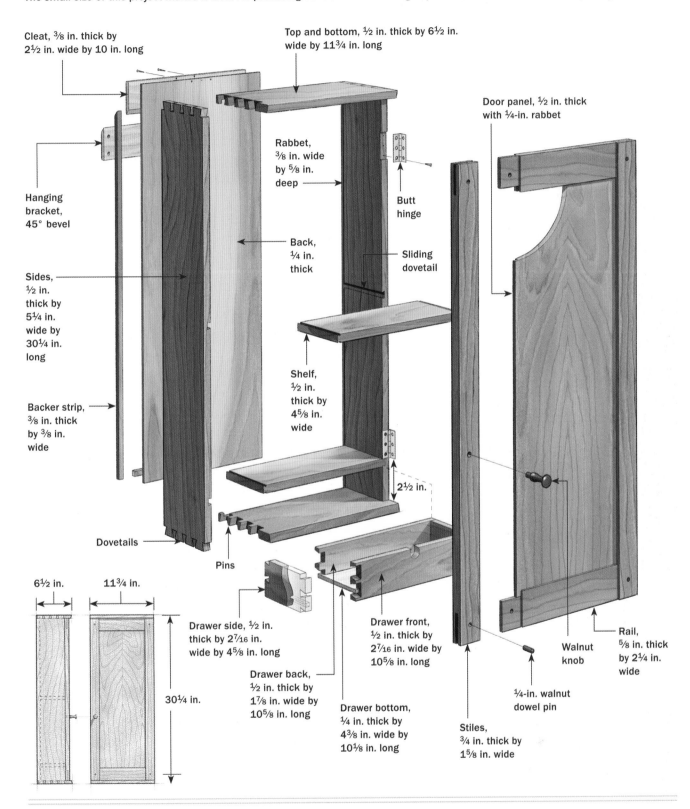

Cleat, ³⁄₈ in. thick by 2½ in. wide by 10 in. long

Top and bottom, ½ in. thick by 6½ in. wide by 11¾ in. long

Door panel, ½ in. thick with ¼-in. rabbet

Hanging bracket, 45° bevel

Rabbet, ³⁄₈ in. wide by ⁵⁄₈ in. deep

Butt hinge

Back, ¼ in. thick

Sliding dovetail

Sides, ½ in. thick by 5¼ in. wide by 30¼ in. long

Shelf, ½ in. thick by 4⁵⁄₈ in. wide

Backer strip, ³⁄₈ in. thick by ³⁄₈ in. wide

2½ in.

Dovetails

Pins

Drawer side, ½ in. thick by 2⁷⁄₁₆ in. wide by 4⁵⁄₈ in. long

Drawer front, ½ in. thick by 2⁷⁄₁₆ in. wide by 10⁵⁄₈ in. long

Walnut knob

Rail, ⁵⁄₈ in. thick by 2¼ in. wide

6½ in.   11¾ in.

Drawer back, ½ in. thick by 1⁷⁄₈ in. wide by 10⁵⁄₈ in. long

Drawer bottom, ¼ in. thick by 4³⁄₈ in. wide by 10⅛ in. long

¼-in. walnut dowel pin

Stiles, ¾ in. thick by 1⁵⁄₈ in. wide

30¼ in.

Lay out the tail centerlines. A single line is all that's needed to mark the tail centerlines (above). On the tablesaw, use the miter gauge with a tall auxiliary fence to make a sawcut at each centerline (right).

Mark the pins with the tails. Use a marking knife to scribe the pin lines on the ends of the top and bottom.

Cut the dovetails on the ends of the case sides. Using the router table equipped with a dovetail bit and a sled to support the stock, the author cuts the dovetails in short order.

Hand saw the pin lines. With the knife lines as a reference, use a dovetail saw to cut along each pin line.

Rout away the waste. After clamping a backer block flush with the top edge of the top or bottom piece, use the router and a straight bit to cut close to the dovetail-saw cut lines.

Trim the excess. After routing, a thin web of wood sometimes remains in the pin. Use a chisel to remove the web and shave away excess stock as needed.

Test the fit. Good-fitting dovetail joints should go together with only moderate hand pressure or a little persuasion from a mallet.

bit to remove in one pass, so I remove a little at the tablesaw first. Holding the stock upright against the miter gauge or crosscut sled, I take a single pass split on each centerline at the tablesaw. The rest of the stock is cut with a single pass through the router bit. Be sure that you clamp the stock to the sled before routing, but don't worry if the tail spacing is slightly irregular; any irregularities in the work will actually do a better job of mimicking traditional hand-cut joinery.

To start cutting pins, use a marking gauge set to the thickness of the sides and mark both ends of the top and bottom to establish the baseline of the dovetails. Clamp the pin stock in the vise, align the ends squarely, and use a marking knife to mark out the pins from the tails. Then trace all the cut lines with a pencil so that they will be easier to see when cutting. Saw the pins by hand, then clean up the excess stock with a router set to cut as deep as the top and bottom are thick.

from the ends, with the other three pins spaced evenly between them.

Using this cutting method, you need only mark the centerline of the cuts and set the router bit to the exact height of the mating stock. This is a lot of material for the router

Sliding dovetails are easy on a router table. The router table and a single dovetail bit are used to cut the dovetail grooves in the sides and the dovetail on each end of the shelves.

No Need to Change the Bit Height

The router-bit height is the same no matter if you are cutting the dovetail groove in a side or the dovetail on the ends of a shelf.

ROUTING THE CASE

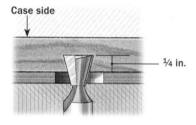

Case side

¼ in.

ROUTING THE SHELVES

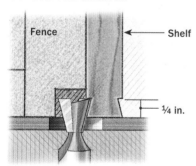

Fence

Shelf

¼ in.

Create the groove. Cut the dovetail groove with the case side flat on the table. Use a pusher board to feed the workpiece and to keep it square to the fence (above). Position the shelves vertically against the fence to cut the tails (left).

To rout out the bulk of the waste and establish a baseline for the tails, use a simple right-angle jig or large backer block clamped to the end of the stock; the block is used to help register the base of the router as you remove the waste.

Once the pins are cut, you'll probably need to trim a little here and there. It's best to trim the pins instead of the tails, which have a tendency to split as you pare them to size. Once trimming is complete, the pins and tails should fit together with firm hand pressure or a few light mallet taps.

If you've got the hinges in hand, go ahead and mortise the sides of the case to accept the hinges. You could do this later by hand, but it's easier to do now with a router.

Sliding dovetails secure the shelves

At this point, you're ready to cut the sliding dovetails that hold the shelves. Again, start by marking out the centerlines of the shelf locations on the case sides. It's a good idea to remove a little of the stock at the tablesaw before routing.

Cut the dovetail grooves first, then assemble the case

Because this is such a small cabinet, I cut the dovetail grooves on the router table. Use the same bit you used to dovetail the carcase. Position the bit in the router table so that about ¼ in. is exposed, and use a square backer board. The pusher board not only holds the case sides square to the fence, it prevents tearout as you rout the tails. Once the dovetail grooves are cut on the case sides, you can assemble the case. Be sure to glue it on a flat surface. After the clamps go on, double-check to make sure the assembly is square.

Cut the shelves to length and rout the dovetails on each end

With the case assembled, mark the shelf length directly from the case. Measure for a snug fit. Use the router table to cut the tail on each end of each shelf. There's no need to change the height setting from the dovetail-groove cut made earlier in the case sides.

Adjust the router fence so that only a small edge of the bit is exposed. Rout the tails on the ends by taking a pass on each face using the same jig you used to rout the dovetails

on the case. Use a piece of test stock and adjust the fence in small increments to sneak up on a good fit.

When you're satisfied with the fit, rout each side of the two shelves and slide the shelves into place. A drop of glue at the front and back of each shelf—applied as the shelf slides into the dovetail grooves—is all you need.

Rabbet the case to accept the back

After the case is glued up, I use a rabbeting bit on the router table to cut a ⅜-in.-wide by ⅝-in.-deep rabbet around the back of the case. To minimize the chance of splintering, stop the cut just short of each corner, then complete the rabbet with a bench chisel. Also, it's best to take about three light passes instead of trying to hog off all the stock in one pass.

The back is nothing more than a ¼-in.-thick panel glued and brad-nailed to the center of the top, bottom, and shelves. The back must be free to expand and contract with changes in humidity, so limit the glue to an area about 2 in. wide. Small strips of ⅜-in.-sq. stock are glued to the sides of the rabbets on the back of the case to secure the panel.

Mount case to wall with cleats

I used a simple two-piece cleat to hang the cabinet (see "Cherry Cabinet," on p. 119). When the cabinet is hung, the pieces interlock for a tight fit against the wall.

Attach one piece to the cabinet so that it butts against the underside of the case top. Use a couple of screws spaced about 2½ in. apart and drive them into the back edge of the cabinet top. Apply a coat of glue between the screws.

Quick door frames on the tablesaw. With each stile and rail connected by a unique version of the mortise-and-tenon called a bridle joint, the door frame enjoys plenty of strength and good looks. To start, cut the tenon shoulders on the rails. After grooving the frame members and mortising the stiles, use the tablesaw to establish the tenon length on each rail.

Add the shelves. After the case is glued and clamped, the shelves are slid into the grooves. For easier assembly, the author applies glue to the back half of the grooves and the front half of the dovetails.

Shadow lines make a simple door interesting

To build the door, the frame is grooved first at the tablesaw and then the joinery is cut on the tablesaw using a tenoning jig. The jig can be either aftermarket or shopmade. I cut the open mortises on the stiles first, then cut the rail tenons to fit.

When the joinery has been cut, plane down the front face of the rails an extra ⅛ in. so that they will be slightly inset on the stiles.

The simple flat panel for the door is cut from ½-in.-thick stock, then rabbeted to fit into the frame. Start by gluing the center of

the panel to the center of both rails. Add a few drops of glue to the mortises, then slide the stiles into place on the rails and panel.

Once the door is together, pegging the joints will strengthen the assembly and help frame the cabinet visually. For contrast, I used ¼-in. walnut dowel pins. To add the pegs, simply drill a ¼-in.-dia. hole just shy of the door thickness, then tap a length of dowel into the hole. The excess can be sawn off and then chiseled flush to the front of the door.

After assembling the door, test the fit against the case. If the assembly went to-

Cut the tenon cheeks. With a tenoning jig supporting the rails on end, cut each tenon cheek. The jig also is used to cut mortises on each end of the stiles to accept the tenons.

A dowel pin adds an interesting detail and a little extra strength. Drill a ¼-in.-dia. by ⅝-in.-deep hole in the front face of the door, centered on the bridle joint, then glue a dowel pin into the hole.

gether square, you should have a perfect fit. If necessary, trim it for a tight fit on the case using either a plane or the tablesaw. Because you've already mortised the case for the hinges, all that's left is to cut the mating hinge mortises in the door. I use a router to cut mortises, but a chisel works as well.

Adding a drawer

The lower drawer inside is joined using through-dovetails at both the front and back. You can use the same dovetailing method you used for the case.

I drilled an off-center ⅞-in.-dia. hole into the drawer face to serve as a finger pull. The hard edges on the finger pull are softened with a knife, and the whittled surfaces are a nice surprise when someone opens the drawer for the first time. Without fail, they pull out the drawer and take a closer look. That closer look is as near to a trophy as a woodworker gets.

A Better Way to Build Wall Cabinets

GARRETT HACK

I made this nice little wall-hung cabinet to hold tools, but it could easily find a spot inside a home and hold small knickknacks. What's interesting about this project is the uncommon way I build the case. The process is efficient, and it yields a strong and very attractive piece with a lot of room for design variations.

The main joints are sliding dovetails, which are rock solid and easily made with a tablesaw and router. Using sliding dovetails forces me to inset the top and bottom of the cabinet, but that works to my advantage, as you'll see.

Also, I use an unusual face-frame variation, which blends more seamlessly with the case. Basically, I cut a deep rabbet in the front edges of the case and glue the stiles into that rabbet. That leaves the glueline very close to the corner, where I can disguise it easily with a chamfer, a bead, or a bit of banding, for a variety of looks. Note that the rails are added later, simply glued to the top and bottom of the case. These also act as blocking for any moldings you want to add.

You might ask, why have a face frame at all? The first reason is that the sides are thin and a face frame allows you to create whatever thickness looks best at the front edges. Also, it lets you run through-dadoes for the shelves. Without a face frame, you would have to cut stopped dadoes to create a clean look at the front. Finally, it is easier to cut hinge mortises in the face-frame stiles while they are loose than it is to cut them in the sides themselves.

The design is best for hanging cabinets, but it works for floor-standing cabinets as well. The "ears" (the part of the sides that extends above the sliding dovetails) can be as short as ¾ in. and hidden behind a molding. Or an overhanging top can be added.

Banding determines the cabinet width

I often add a banding under the crown molding to serve as a transition between the molding and the case. It might seem like an unusual place to start, but to get the cabinet width and the length of the top and bottom pieces, I need to know this banding length. The idea is to end up with a uniform black square on each end of the banding.

So after I ripped up the black and white pieces (ebony and holly) on the tablesaw, I laid out the sandwich and then used it to tick off the full banding length on a story stick. Then, to get the width of the cabinet, I had to subtract the slight overhang of the banding. Last, I marked the length of the crosspieces on the story stick. Because the dadoes and dovetails are the same depth, you can cut the shelves, top, and bottom to the same length with the same setup—another bonus.

(continued on p. 131)

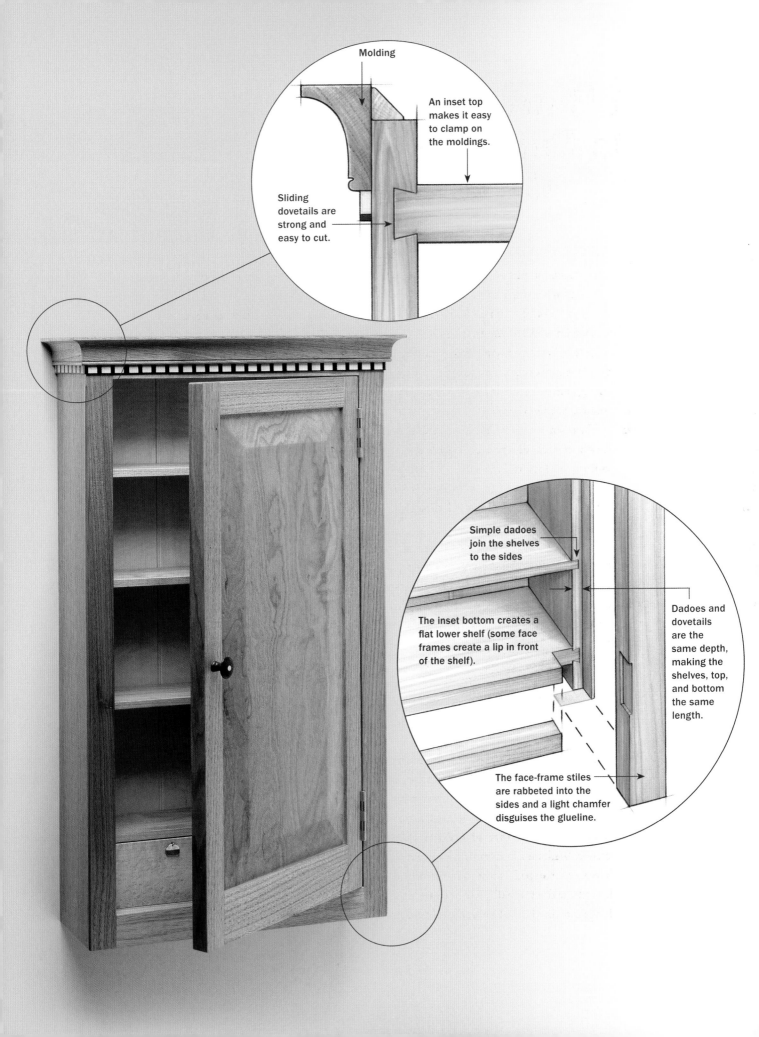

Molding

An inset top
makes it easy
to clamp on
the moldings.

Sliding
dovetails are
strong and
easy to cut.

Simple dadoes
join the shelves
to the sides

The inset bottom creates a
flat lower shelf (some face
frames create a lip in front
of the shelf).

Dadoes and
dovetails
are the
same depth,
making the
shelves, top,
and bottom
the same
length.

The face-frame stiles
are rabbeted into the
sides and a light chamfer
disguises the glueline.

Wall Cabinet

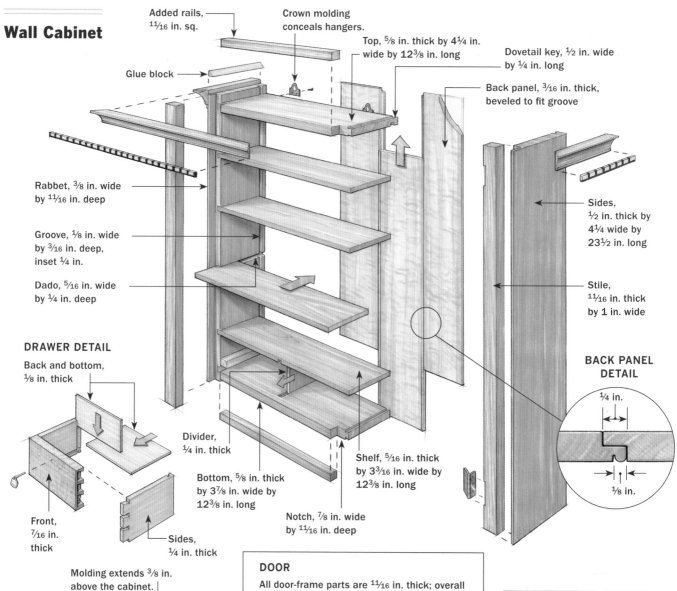

Added rails,
$^{11}/_{16}$ in. sq.

Crown molding
conceals hangers.

Top, $^{5}/_{8}$ in. thick by $4^{1}/_{4}$ in.
wide by $12^{3}/_{8}$ in. long

Dovetail key, $^{1}/_{2}$ in. wide
by $^{1}/_{4}$ in. long

Glue block

Back panel, $^{3}/_{16}$ in. thick,
beveled to fit groove

Rabbet, $^{3}/_{8}$ in. wide
by $^{11}/_{16}$ in. deep

Groove, $^{1}/_{8}$ in. wide
by $^{3}/_{16}$ in. deep,
inset $^{1}/_{4}$ in.

Dado, $^{5}/_{16}$ in. wide
by $^{1}/_{4}$ in. deep

Sides,
$^{1}/_{2}$ in. thick by
$4^{1}/_{4}$ wide by
$23^{1}/_{2}$ in. long

Stile,
$^{11}/_{16}$ in. thick
by 1 in. wide

DRAWER DETAIL

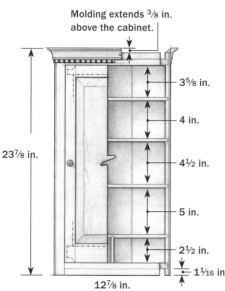

Back and bottom,
$^{1}/_{8}$ in. thick

Front,
$^{7}/_{16}$ in.
thick

Sides,
$^{1}/_{4}$ in. thick

Divider,
$^{1}/_{4}$ in. thick

Bottom, $^{5}/_{8}$ in. thick by $3^{7}/_{8}$ in. wide by
$12^{3}/_{8}$ in. long

Shelf, $^{5}/_{16}$ in. thick
by $3^{3}/_{16}$ in. wide by
$12^{3}/_{8}$ in. long

Notch, $^{7}/_{8}$ in. wide
by $^{11}/_{16}$ in. deep

BACK PANEL DETAIL

$^{1}/_{4}$ in.

$^{1}/_{8}$ in.

Molding extends $^{3}/_{8}$ in.
above the cabinet.

$23^{7}/_{8}$ in.

$3^{5}/_{8}$ in.

4 in.

$4^{1}/_{2}$ in.

5 in.

$2^{1}/_{2}$ in.

$1^{1}/_{16}$ in.

$12^{7}/_{8}$ in.

DOOR

All door-frame parts are $^{11}/_{16}$ in. thick; overall
dimensions are $10^{5}/_{8}$ in. by $20^{5}/_{8}$ in.

Stiles, $1^{1}/_{8}$ in. wide

Top rail,
$1^{1}/_{4}$ in. wide

Groove, $^{1}/_{4}$ in.
by $^{1}/_{4}$ in.

Panel, $^{7}/_{16}$ in.
thick, with
$1^{1}/_{4}$-in.-
wide bevel

Bottom rail,
2 in. wide

Tenons, $^{1}/_{4}$ in.
thick by $^{7}/_{8}$ in. long

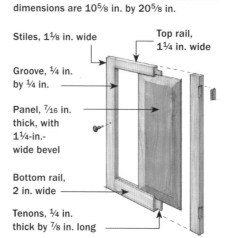

**Size the case to the
banding.** To ensure that the
banding ends with black stripes
on each end, mill the banding
stock first and tick off the exact
case width on a story stick.

Perfect alignment, guaranteed. To be sure all the dadoes and dovetail slots align perfectly, tape the sides together (above) when you cut the joints. Start by cutting the sides to length on the tablesaw, then install a dado blade to cut the shelf dadoes (right). Cut the same 5/16-in.-wide dadoes at the sliding-dovetail locations. This will clear a path for the dovetail bit.

Rout the dovetail slots and keys. With the case sides still taped together, set a dovetail bit at the same height as the dadoes and rout the slots (far left). Without moving the bit, adjust the fence to cut the keys in the case top and bottom (left).

A few more steps. After grooving the sides and top for the back panel, rabbet the sides for the face frame.

Shelves first. Start by gluing the shelves into their dadoes and clamping them in place (above). Slide the case top and bottom into place from the rear (right).

Face frame comes next. Check the fit of the face-frame stiles and then glue them into their rabbets (left). Complete the face frame simply by gluing rails to the case top and bottom (right).

Install the divider and back. Press the divider into place (above) and plane it flush after the glue has dried. The back consists of three shiplapped boards that are beveled to fit the grooves in the case sides and top. Slide them in from the bottom (right) and nail them to the shelves.

TIP It's easier to cut the mortises for the hinges in the stile before gluing it into the case.

Cut the joinery

Start with the sides of the case. Leave them a bit long and tape them together, as shown in the photos on p. 129. Mark the finished length of the sides and lay out the dadoes for all the crosspieces (even the sliding dovetails start out as dadoes). After cutting those dadoes, move to the router table to turn the dadoes for the top and bottom of the case into sliding dovetails. The next step is to cut the dovetail keys on the top and bottom of the case. Run both sides of the dovetail past the bit and creep up on a nice fit. The dovetail key should slide partway in with only a small amount of pressure.

Now you can rabbet the sides and notch the top and bottom of the case for the face-frame stiles. Plane the stiles to fit perfectly later.

A raised back in three pieces

You can put any type of back into a cabinet like this, but I use a three-piece solid-wood back, shiplapped together. This lets me distribute the wood movement over four gaps instead of two. It also allows me to add a bead to the joints that looks great inside the cabinet. I beveled the edges to fit into a small groove in the sides and top, making the back look like a raised panel.

Finish off the shelves

Now you can complete the shelves. They've been cut to final length, but should still be a little thick. Take time now to plane them by hand or power to fit their dadoes.

I add a vertical divider under the bottom shelf. That allows for two small drawers or one drawer and an open shelf. Note that the bottom dado for the divider doesn't extend all the way to the front, so it must be a stopped cut, made with a router.

How to make decorative banding

Glue up alternating strips of dark and light wood into a sandwich. Surface one side and crosscut the sandwich into ¼-in.-thick strips (1). Rip the crosscuts into ³⁄₁₆-in.-thick strips on the bandsaw (2). Clean up the saw-marks with a block plane.

Starting at a corner, glue the banding in place one segment at a time (3). Rub a block of wood over the banding to seat it in place (4). No clamping is necessary. I added a thin strip of ebony to the bottom edge of the banding to create a pleasing border. Again, simply rub it on to attach it (5).

Glue up in stages

Make sure all the parts are marked clearly so you know where they go and which end is which. Start with the shelves, then do the face frames. Move on to the divider and back. Use only a small amount of glue on the beginning of the dovetail slot and key. Too much will cause the joint to swell and bind. Check the case with a square as you assemble it.

Finishing touches make the difference

There are lots of ways to finish off the top of a wall cabinet. It needs something; otherwise, it looks too much like a box. I used a cove molding, with that little banding just below it. One advantage of this case construction is the extra pieces (I call them *ears*) that stick up beyond the sliding dovetail to give it strength. They are the perfect place to clamp

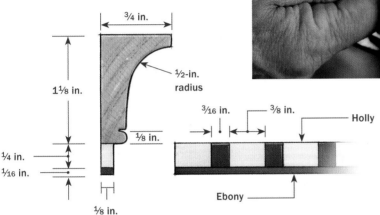

Add the molding. The ears that extend beyond the dovetailed case top provide a convenient clamping surface for the molding (right). A bead, cut with a scratch stock (above), is a nice transition for the banding.

Molding Detail

¾ in.

1⅛ in.

½-in. radius

⅛ in.

¼ in.

¹⁄₁₆ in.

⅛ in.

³⁄₁₆ in.

⅜ in.

Holly

Ebony

Begin the chamfer below the molding. The author begins a stopped chamfer ½ in. below the molding. He starts the chamfer with a chisel, bevel down (top right), and continues it to the bottom of the case with a block plane (above). Deepen the chamfer until one edge lines up with the glueline.

those moldings. They were so short that I wasn't worried about cross-grain movement. With a deeper cabinet, I might screw them on from the inside, running the back screws through slotted holes. Of course, the front molding can always be glued on with no issues.

You can use any method you like for the door, drawer, and even the back of the cabinet. This approach to construction is very versatile and works for cabinets of all sizes with all kinds of molding and decoration. That's why I love it.

Another Corner Option

Cut a shallower rabbet in the case sides and fill the resulting space with a banding.

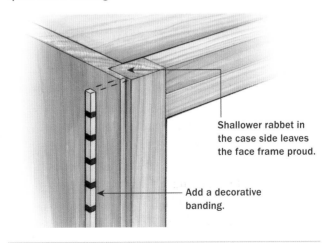

Shallower rabbet in the case side leaves the face frame proud.

Add a decorative banding.

A Vanity Cabinet

MARIO RODRIGUEZ

Browsing at a country flea market one weekend, I came across a vendor selling interesting architectural pieces. There were fireplace mantels, stained-glass panels, doors, and some odd lengths of ornate moldings. What really caught my eye, though, was a bathroom wall cabinet of Victorian vintage. It was simple and graceful, with a soaring cornice and nearly perfect proportions. Miraculously, it still wore its original finish. Over the years the cabinet had developed a deep, rusty color and a wonderful patina, punctuated by a brass Victorian cupboard latch. This was a piece worth copying.

I took some measurements, snapped a few photos, and then returned to my shop to draw up plans for a similar piece. This cabinet is the result. I made it out of quartersawn white oak. The ray-fleck grain patterns give a nice flair to the simple lines of the cabinet. What's really nifty is how the mirrored door is made. I assembled the parts with slip tenons—nothing revolutionary—but before cutting the joinery, I rabbeted the pieces for the mirror. This method creates half-lap joints and a perfectly square recess for the mirror without any need for chisel work in the corners.

This piece is a popular class at my school, and I understand why. It doesn't take long to build and it adds a handmade touch to any bathroom.

No-fuss shelf supports. To add longevity, the author chose shelf pins that are housed in hollow sleeves. The easiest way to set the sleeves flush is to use a special punch (www. leevalley.com, 00K61.02), as shown.

Shelf edge detail. The two adjustable shelves have a decorative bead routed on their front edges.

Mirrored Vanity Shines

This white-oak vanity cabinet is a warm departure from manufactured cabinets, giving your bath a handmade touch. The case joinery is simple, and the door assembly makes installing a mirror a breeze. The custom cove molding on top is all done at the tablesaw.

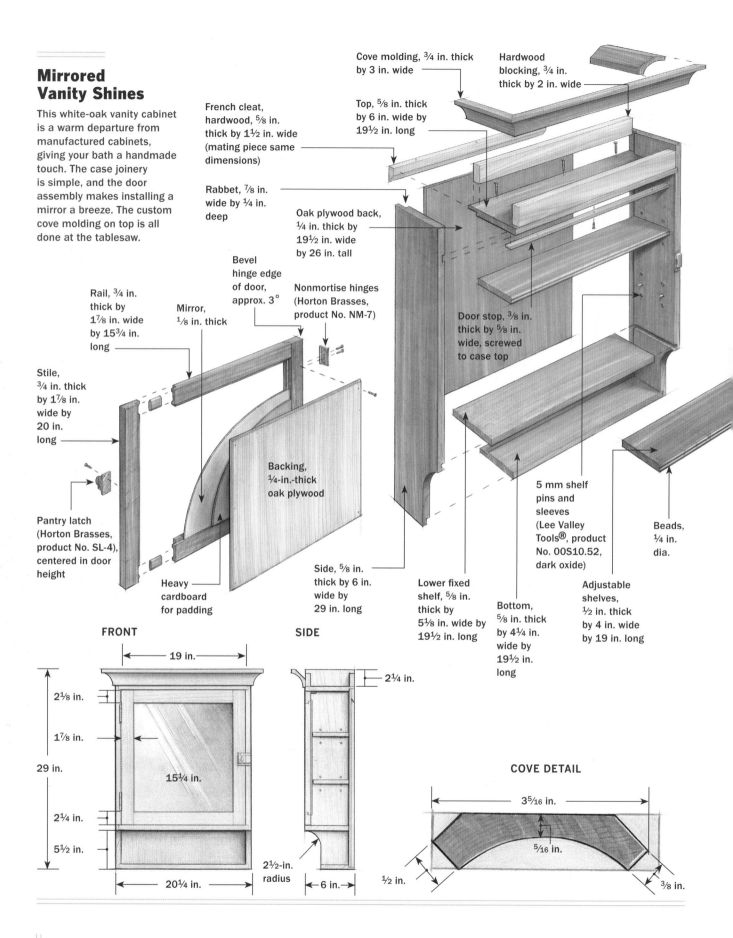

Cove molding, 3/4 in. thick by 3 in. wide

Hardwood blocking, 3/4 in. thick by 2 in. wide

French cleat, hardwood, 5/8 in. thick by 1½ in. wide (mating piece same dimensions)

Top, 5/8 in. thick by 6 in. wide by 19½ in. long

Rabbet, 7/8 in. wide by 1/4 in. deep

Oak plywood back, 1/4 in. thick by 19½ in. wide by 26 in. tall

Bevel hinge edge of door, approx. 3°

Nonmortise hinges (Horton Brasses, product No. NM-7)

Rail, 3/4 in. thick by 1 7/8 in. wide by 15 3/4 in. long

Mirror, 1/8 in. thick

Stile, 3/4 in. thick by 1 7/8 in. wide by 20 in. long

Door stop, 3/8 in. thick by 5/8 in. wide, screwed to case top

Backing, 1/4-in.-thick oak plywood

Pantry latch (Horton Brasses, product No. SL-4), centered in door height

Heavy cardboard for padding

Side, 5/8 in. thick by 6 in. wide by 29 in. long

Lower fixed shelf, 5/8 in. thick by 5 1/8 in. wide by 19½ in. long

5 mm shelf pins and sleeves (Lee Valley Tools®, product No. 00S10.52, dark oxide)

Beads, 1/4 in. dia.

Bottom, 5/8 in. thick by 4 1/4 in. wide by 19½ in. long

Adjustable shelves, 1/2 in. thick by 4 in. wide by 19 in. long

FRONT

19 in.

2 1/8 in.

1 7/8 in.

29 in.

15 1/4 in.

2 1/4 in.

5½ in.

20 1/4 in.

SIDE

2 1/4 in.

2½-in. radius

6 in.

COVE DETAIL

3 5/16 in.

5/16 in.

1/2 in.

3/8 in.

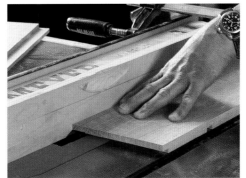

Dadoes and bottom rabbet. After cutting the rabbet for the bottom, cut the dadoes for the top and fixed middle shelf (far left). Any tearout on the back will be removed when you cut the rabbets for the back panel and French cleat (left). Bury the blade in a sacrificial fence when rabbeting.

Bandsaw the bottom curve. The cutout at the bottom of the cabinet gives the case a slimmer look. Smooth the bandsaw marks with a spindle sander, a spokeshave, or curved sanding blocks.

Case joinery comes first

The joinery is really straightforward, and it's all done at the tablesaw using a dado set. However, all the joints are visible, so make sure they're clean and tight. Once the case joinery is done, use a bandsaw to cut out the arc on the bottom of each side. This arc gives the cabinet a slimmer look and provides more clearance to reach items stored on the bottom shelf.

Plane and sand all the parts, then you're ready to glue up the case. After assembly, drill for the shelf pins that will support the adjustable shelves. To ensure the shelf-pin holes were aligned side to side, I made a drilling template out of ¼-in.-thick plywood. I clamped it to one side of the cabinet, drilled the holes, and then slid it to the other side to drill the others.

Clamp it up. After planing and sanding the case parts, glue them up. Do a dry run first to make sure that everything comes together cleanly and squarely.

Cove Cutting on the Tablesaw

You can't cut a cove this big with a router bit, but a time-tested tablesaw technique handles it easily. Take time to set up the cut accurately and take light passes to creep up on the profile.

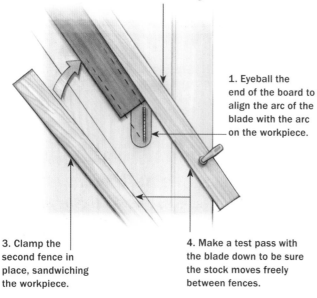

2. Mark the approach angle on the tablesaw top and clamp the first fence along that mark.

1. Eyeball the end of the board to align the arc of the blade with the arc on the workpiece.

3. Clamp the second fence in place, sandwiching the workpiece.

4. Make a test pass with the blade down to be sure the stock moves freely between fences.

First pass. After clamping both fences securely, make a test pass with the blade below the table, just to be sure that the stock slides without binding. Then raise the blade to 1/16 in. high and make the first pass. Use a push stick or pad in your back hand and stop your front hand short of passing over the blade.

Height, then angle. Raise the blade to meet the apex, or high point, of the arc (above). Now angle the fences so that the ends of the arc align with the leading and trailing teeth of the blade. Mark that angle on the tablesaw top and then clamp the fences in place (right).

The final cuts. Raise the blade in 1/16-in. increments until you get within about 1/6 in. of the profile mark. Then make lighter passes, in 1/32-in. increments, until you hit the mark.

Trim the molding. Now make the 45° trim cuts on both edges to finish off the molding.

Better way to miter molding. The author assembles the molding before attaching it to the cabinet. This way he is ensured of tight miters with no gaps. To turn the compound-angle miters into simple 45° cuts, he supports the work in a cradle. Make both left and right cuts in the front fence first, and then use those kerfs to line up the molding cuts.

Clean up before mitering. Use a gooseneck scraper and a curved sanding block to remove the tablesaw marks.

Cut the cove for the cornice

Making your own molding is a great way to add a custom touch. Most can be done with a router, but the cove molding for this piece is too large for standard bits, so I used a slick technique on the tablesaw (see "Cove Cutting on the Tablesaw" on the facing page). I passed the stock over the spinning blade at an angle, guiding it between two fences clamped to the saw top.

You don't need a complicated formula to determine the angle of the fences. Simply raise the blade to the full height of the cut and angle the stock until the ends of the arc align with the leading and trailing teeth of the blade. Now clamp the two fences on either side of the stock, raise the blade to about 1⁄16 in., and run the stock over it. Raise the blade in 1⁄16-in. increments with each

Cradle Makes Compound-Angle Cuts Easy

With this cradle you can make a compound-angle cut with a simple 45° miter cut on the chopsaw. The key is that the molding is held at its installed angle. All parts are plywood, except for the front fence, which is poplar.

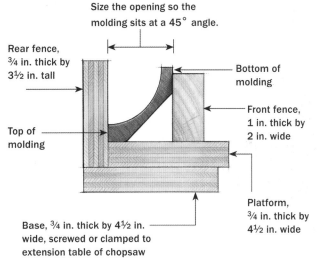

Size the opening so the molding sits at a 45° angle.

Rear fence, 3⁄4 in. thick by 3 1⁄2 in. tall

Top of molding

Bottom of molding

Front fence, 1 in. thick by 2 in. wide

Platform, 3⁄4 in. thick by 4 1⁄2 in. wide

Base, 3⁄4 in. thick by 4 1⁄2 in. wide, screwed or clamped to extension table of chopsaw

pass. As you approach the finished profile, take smaller, 1⁄32-in. bites, which will leave a slightly smoother surface that will be easier to clean up.

After finishing the cove profile, make a series of 45° edge cuts on the tablesaw. These cuts project the cove molding at a 45° angle from the cabinet, which looks

From cradle to case. After carefully cutting the miters, using the case as a guide for the length of the front piece, cut the side moldings to final length. Assemble the sections on the bench using glue and a pin nailer (left). Let the assembly dry, slide it onto the top of the case (below), and nail it in place.

attractive and presents a solid and stable surface for installation.

Prebuilt miters stay tight

Most people fit and miter cornice moldings right on the case, but it can be difficult to get gap-free miters. I have a better way. I preassemble the moldings, ensuring that the corners are tight, then attach the entire assembly to the case. Attaching an assembled cornice lets me build it square with tight miters, and then coax it into position.

The cornice requires a compound-angle miter. It's common to make this cut with a tablesaw or compound-miter saw. With the tablesaw you need to angle both the workpiece and the blade; with the compound-miter saw you need to angle the blade in two directions and find a way to support the

Simple but Sturdy Door Joints

The door is assembled with slip tenons. But before cutting the mortises, the author cuts the rabbets for the mirror. The process creates a perfectly square recess plus half laps at the joints.

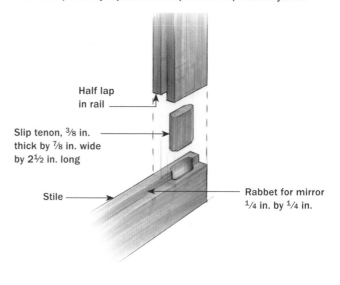

Half lap in rail

Slip tenon, 3/8 in. thick by 7/8 in. wide by 2 1/2 in. long

Stile

Rabbet for mirror 1/4 in. by 1/4 in.

Clever Jig for Mortising

This simple shopmade jig makes it easy to center a 3/8-in.-wide by 7/8-in.-long mortise on both the rails and stiles, using a 3/4-in.-O.D. bushing and 3/8-in. spiral bit.

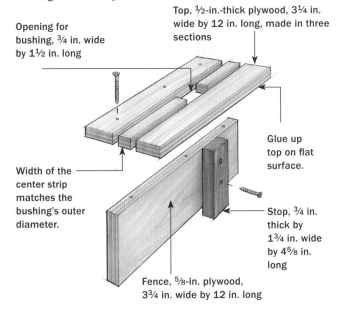

Opening for bushing, 3/4 in. wide by 1 1/2 in. long

Top, 1/2-in.-thick plywood, 3 1/4 in. wide by 12 in. long, made in three sections

Width of the center strip matches the bushing's outer diameter.

Glue up top on flat surface.

Stop, 3/4 in. thick by 1 3/4 in. wide by 4 5/8 in. long

Fence, 5/8-in. plywood, 3 3/4 in. wide by 12 in. long

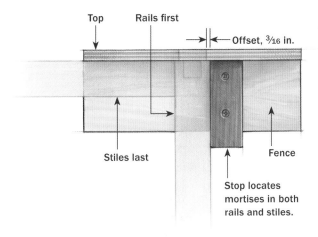

Top

Rails first

Offset, 3/16 in.

Stiles last

Fence

Stop locates mortises in both rails and stiles.

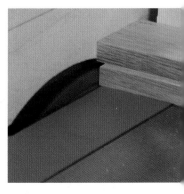

Make way for the mirror. Use the same dado set to rabbet the stiles and rails (left) and to cut half laps in the rails (right).

Rout the rail first. Clamp the jig in a vise, with the bottom of the rail tight against the stop and with the end tight to the top, then rout using a 3/8-in. spiral bit and guide bushing.

Rout for Loose Tenons

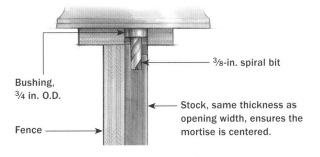

Bushing, 3/4 in. O.D.

Fence

3/8-in. spiral bit

Stock, same thickness as opening width, ensures the mortise is centered.

molding. Once again, I have an easier way. I cut the miters on a simple chopsaw, with the workpiece nestled in a cradle that holds it at the correct angle (see "Cradle Makes Compound-Angle Cuts Easy" on p. 139).

After mitering and attaching the crown, install the back panel and French cleat.

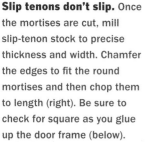

Stiles next. Butt the end of the stile tightly against the stop and tight to the top.

Slip tenons don't slip. Once the mortises are cut, mill slip-tenon stock to precise thickness and width. Chamfer the edges to fit the round mortises and then chop them to length (right). Be sure to check for square as you glue up the door frame (below).

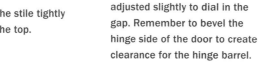

Hinges. Nonmortise hinges are easy to install and can be adjusted slightly to dial in the gap. Remember to bevel the hinge side of the door to create clearance for the hinge barrel.

Mirror

The plywood backer over the mirror is cut from the same ¼-in. oak plywood as the case back.

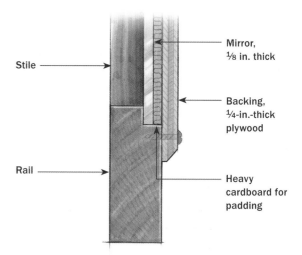

Stile →

Rail →

→ Mirror, ⅛ in. thick

→ Backing, ¼-in.-thick plywood

→ Heavy cardboard for padding

Mirrored door is easy

could have made a traditional door frame, with mortise-and-tenon joints, and then routed out a rabbet for the mirror. But routing the rabbet after assembling the door often results in tearout when you change direction. It also can be difficult to support the router on the frame without tipping, which leads to a bumpy or wavy cut. And you have to square up the corners with chisels afterward. Instead, I cut the rabbets for the mirror in the rails and stiles first, and I joined the parts using slip tenons. This gives me a strong door with a perfectly square rabbet for the mirror.

For an easy door installation, I chose non-mortised hinges from Horton Brasses (www. horton-brasses.com). When installed, these hinges allow a generous ¹⁄₁₆-in. reveal. After cutting the door to size, allowing ¹⁄₁₆ in. spacing all around, you have to cut a 3° back bevel on the hinge side/edge of the door to give clearance for the door to open and close without binding. Once the door is hung, install the pantry latch and strike, and then the door stop.

Now cut the mirror and cardboard backing to fit the door rabbet. Then cut and screw the plywood backing over those pieces.

For the finish, you need to choose something that will hold up in a steamy environment. I warmed the oak with amber shellac, then sprayed the cabinet with lacquer. If you don't have a sprayer, any wipe-on varnish or oil/poly mixture will work.

Quick, Sturdy Bookcase

MARTIN MILKOVITS

In my home, bookcases show up in every room, serving not only as places to store our growing collection of books but also as places to display art and other items of interest. This butternut-and-maple bookcase is a versatile piece, big enough to hold a good number of books and/or collectibles while small enough to fit in almost any room.

The design is understated, with bracket feet and gentle curves along the tops of the sides, and maple back boards contrasting softly with butternut sides and shelves.

But you can use this construction method to build a bookcase in any style. The shelves are attached to the sides with sliding dovetails, which provide a mechanical connection that will never pull apart. Sliding dovetails also are used to connect cabinet tops to bottoms, to join vertical partitions to shelves, to attach molding to case sides, to connect breadboard ends to tabletops, and to attach drawer fronts to sides. In this case, I stopped the dovetails for a clean look on the front of the piece. The back boards are shiplapped to allow for wood movement.

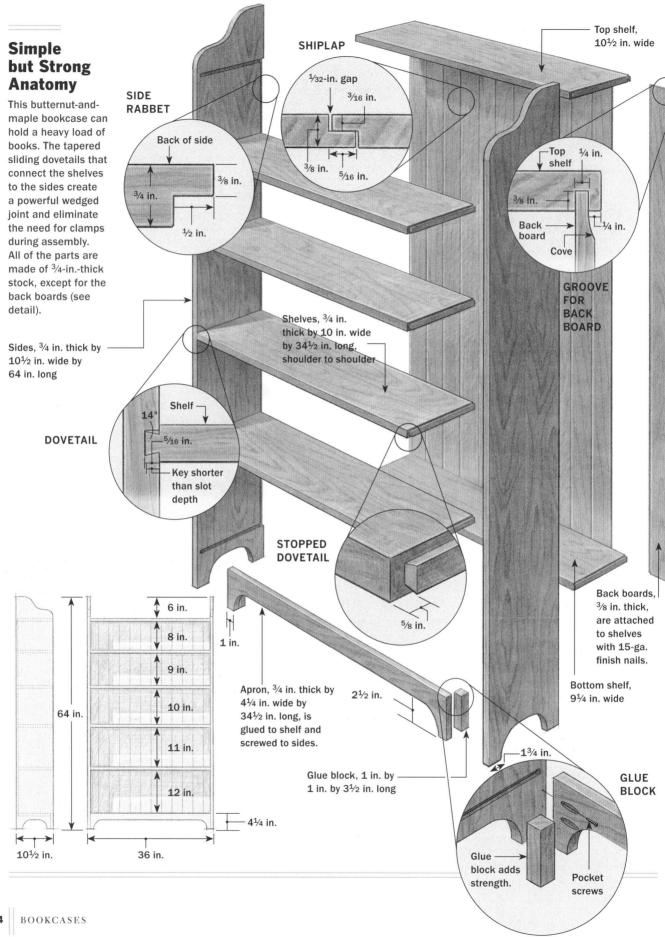

Simple but Strong Anatomy

This butternut-and-maple bookcase can hold a heavy load of books. The tapered sliding dovetails that connect the shelves to the sides create a powerful wedged joint and eliminate the need for clamps during assembly. All of the parts are made of ¾-in.-thick stock, except for the back boards (see detail).

Sides, ¾ in. thick by 10½ in. wide by 64 in. long

SIDE RABBET

Back of side

¾ in.

⅜ in.

½ in.

SHIPLAP

1/32-in. gap

3/16 in.

⅜ in.

5/16 in.

Top shelf, 10½ in. wide

Top shelf

¼ in.

⅜ in.

Back board

¼ in.

Cove

GROOVE FOR BACK BOARD

Shelves, ¾ in. thick by 10 in. wide by 34½ in. long, shoulder to shoulder

DOVETAIL

14°

Shelf

5/16 in.

Key shorter than slot depth

STOPPED DOVETAIL

5/8 in.

Apron, ¾ in. thick by 4¼ in. wide by 34½ in. long, is glued to shelf and screwed to sides.

1 in.

2½ in.

Glue block, 1 in. by 1 in. by 3½ in. long

Back boards, ⅜ in. thick, are attached to shelves with 15-ga. finish nails.

Bottom shelf, 9¼ in. wide

1¾ in.

GLUE BLOCK

Glue block adds strength.

Pocket screws

64 in.

6 in.

8 in.

9 in.

10 in.

11 in.

12 in.

4¼ in.

10½ in.

36 in.

Tapered Slots in Two Steps

To ensure consistent results, the slots for each shelf are routed using a long fence and a plywood cleat.
After the first pass, add a shim between the fence and cleat, then use the same router setup to taper the slot.

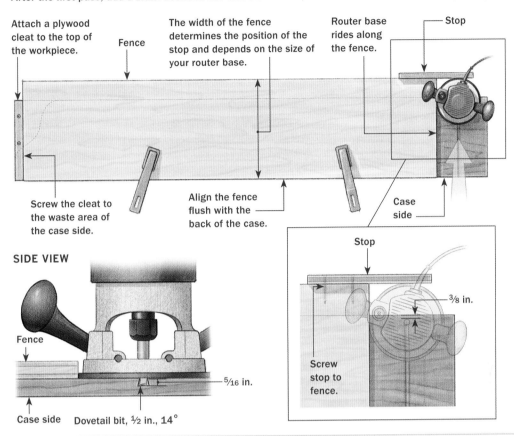

Attach a plywood cleat to the top of the workpiece.

Fence

The width of the fence determines the position of the stop and depends on the size of your router base.

Router base rides along the fence.

Stop

Screw the cleat to the waste area of the case side.

Align the fence flush with the back of the case.

Case side

SIDE VIEW

Fence

Case side

Dovetail bit, ½ in., 14°

⁵⁄₁₆ in.

Stop

Screw stop to fence.

³⁄₈ in.

First pass. Attach a cleat to each case side. Screw the plywood cleat to the top of the inside case sides and perfectly square to the edges. Place screws in areas that will be wasted away when you profile the ends.

Clamp the fence to the workpiece. Align the front edge of the fence flush with the back of the case side and tight against the cleat at the top.

Rout the slot. Holding the router tight against the fence for control, cut until you reach the stop. Let the bit stop spinning before backing it out of the slot or you could ruin the cut.

Second pass. Shim out the back side. Place the shim between the fence and the cleat. Veneer tape is the perfect thickness (1/32 in.) to create the desired taper.

Reclamp and rerout. With the shim in place and the fence reclamped, run the router through the slot to add the taper.

Trim the fence. After routing both slots for the bottom shelf, cut the fence down to repeat the process on the next set of slots.

ADD A SHIM TO TAPER THE SLOTS

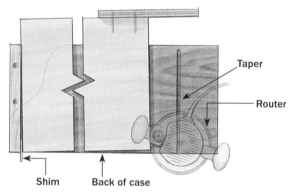

Taper

Router

Shim   Back of case

Why taper the dovetail?

A sliding dovetail has two parts: the slot and the dovetail key. Here the slots are routed into the case sides and the keys are cut on the ends of the shelf. When you use this joint in wide stock, binding is a common headache during glue-up. The joint goes halfway home, then the glue makes the wood swell and the joint seizes. That's why I taper the joint slightly toward the front of the case. The taper—cut on one side of the slot and on the corresponding face of the key—makes it easy to slide the shelf in from the back without binding and creates a wedging action in front as the shelf is tapped home.

The amount of taper is not that critical as long as it is consistent. I keep it to about 1/32 in. (about as thick as three business cards) per 10 in. of board width. With a taper like this, the joint can be almost completely as-sembled for trial fitting and can be driven home with a few mallet blows.

Router method simplifies complex joint

Tapered sliding dovetails can be cut by hand, using saws and chisels, but this method can be imprecise and time-consuming. I prefer to use a router and a few simple jigs to do the job. The method is clean and allows you to dial in the fit of each joint. To avoid confusion, be sure to label mating parts as you work.

Cut slots with a handheld router

For strength, the slot should be no deeper than half the thickness of the side. Likewise, the thin part of the key should be at least half the thickness of the shelf, and the length at least one-third the thickness of the shelf.

First, screw a ¾-in.-thick plywood cleat to the top of the case sides. Mark the shelf locations on each side, then make a ¾-in.-thick plywood fence to locate the slots in both sides. Cut the fence to a length that aligns the router bit with the lower shelf location and rip it to a width that will place the router bit ⅜ in. from the front of the side. Screw

a stop to the business end of the fence and clamp the assembly in place (see "Tapered Slots in Two Steps" on p. 145).

Set the router to make a ⁵⁄₁₆-in.-deep cut and rout the slot across the side until you reach the stop. Next, remove the fence and place a shim between the rear edge of the cleat and the rear edge of the fence. Re-clamp the fence in place, then pass the router through the slot to create the taper along the bottom edge. Repeat this operation in the opposite side of the case. Once you have both slots for the bottom shelf routed and tapered, trim the fence to cut slots for the next higher shelf and repeat all of the previous steps.

Now is a good time to cut the bracket feet on the bottom of the sides as well as the profile on top. Clean up those edges before proceeding.

Taper the Dovetail Keys

The keys are cut and tapered at the router table using the same bit that cut the slots, adjusted so that its height is a hair under the slot depth. Use a tall auxiliary fence to keep the long workpieces stable.

Shim the rear edge of the shelf bottom and rout both sides of the shelf end.

Front of shelf

Tapered edge of key

Straight edge of key

Shim on bottom face of shelf

Test piece gets you started. Take light passes along both edges of a test piece (made from a shelf offcut) until it slides halfway or more into a slot with hand pressure.

Shim out the bottom rear of the shelves. Use a shim of the same thickness used to taper the slots. Veneer tape is great because you can iron it on and take it off easily.

Fine-tune the fit. Keep making hairline passes on the router table to get the key to slide closer to home (top left). To micro-adjust the fit, use a sanding block cut to the same angle as the dovetail bit and attach adhesive-backed P120-grit sandpaper to it (below). The goal is to get the shelf to slide with just hand pressure until it is about 1½ in. from being fully home (below left).

Cut keys on the router table

Place the same bit you used to cut the slots into the router table and set the depth so that it's a hair less (0.005 in. or so) than the depth of the slots. This will create a tiny gap to make the sliding action easier. Using a test piece the same thickness as the shelves, adjust the fence and take light cuts on both sides until the test piece fits about halfway or more into a slot with hand pressure. Once you've reached that point, you are ready to rout the actual shelves.

First, add a shim to the bottom rear of each shelf. The shim should be the same thickness as the shim used to taper the slots. Rout the top side of the key on each end of each shelf. Then flip each shelf to cut the bottom of the keys. At this point, each shelf should slide freely about halfway home but tight after that. To fit the shelves individually, make hairline passes across the top, straight side of each key until the shelf slides to within 1½ in. of being fully home with

Trim ⁵/₈ in. from the front of the key. Use a handsaw to remove most of the waste, and clean up the cut with a sharp chisel.

Push and pound. Stand the sides rear-edge up on an assembly bench. To install each shelf, place a spot of glue inside the corresponding slots near the front edge. Push in the shelf as far as you can by hand and fist, then rap the shelf home with a mallet. When installing the bottom shelf, put the apron in place to serve as a stop. Later you can screw the apron into place.

Nail in the back boards in order. Slide the top edges of the boards into the groove under the top shelf. To avoid misses, mark the shelf locations across the back, then nail each board to each shelf with 15-ga. finish nails.

only hand pressure. Use a small, angled sanding block to dial in the fit.

Next, use a handsaw and a chisel to trim ⅝ in. from the front of the keys. Refine the fit with the sanding block if needed. Now rout a groove under the top shelf, ¼ in. from the back edge, for the back boards. Next, rip the lower shelves to size along their back edges and trim an additional ¾ in. off the front of the bottom shelf to accommodate the apron. Finally, cut the rabbets that hold the back boards.

Glue in shelves, then add back boards

Once you have all the shelves fitted to the sides, the hardest work is done. Now's the time to glue up the case and cut and fit the back boards and apron.

The maple back boards are ripped to random widths no wider than 3½ in. Once the boards are cut to final size, use a raised-panel cove cutter to rout a ¼-in. tongue along their tops. Then rout the rabbets along their sides to create the shiplap.

To glue in the shelves, stand the sides rear-edge up on an assembly bench. Place a spot of glue inside the corresponding slots near the front edge, slide in the shelf as far as you can with hand pressure, then tap the shelf home with a mallet.

After installing the apron and glue blocks, the piece is ready for finishing (the back boards are finished before final installation). For this bookcase, I sprayed on Deft® clear lacquer.

After you have the back boards in place, the bookcase is ready for your collection of Russian nesting dolls.

Cherry and Fir Bookcase

PETER ZUERNER

Several years ago, my sister Cicely was looking for a bookcase that would be attractive, functional, and reasonably easy to move. The piece I designed and built for her is now one of the stock pieces in my furniture shop. I call it, appropriately, Cicely's Bookshelf.

I wanted the bookcase to have a spare and elegant look, so I kept the frame parts to a minimum and elevated the piece off the floor by extending the corner posts to create four short legs. All four edges of the top, along with the front edge of each shelf, were given a generously sized cove to create the illusion of thinner stock. As a result, even when the piece is filled with books, it appears light and graceful.

Choose the wood with care

For me, the first and most important step in any furniture project is the process of selecting the wood. Consistent color and grain are important, and I'm always on the lookout for something interesting. I especially like to incorporate special grain or a natural defect. Not only does an odd grain or a small defect make each piece a bit more unique, it also provides a strong visual connection to the tree from which it evolved. For instance, the piece shown here has a small, sound knot near the front of the lower shelf, about midway across the span.

In this piece, I liked the idea of blending darker cherry with the strong grain of quarter-

Frame-and-Panel Bookcase

The author incorporated frame-and-panel construction in his bookcase, with the mortise and tenon accounting for most of the joinery.

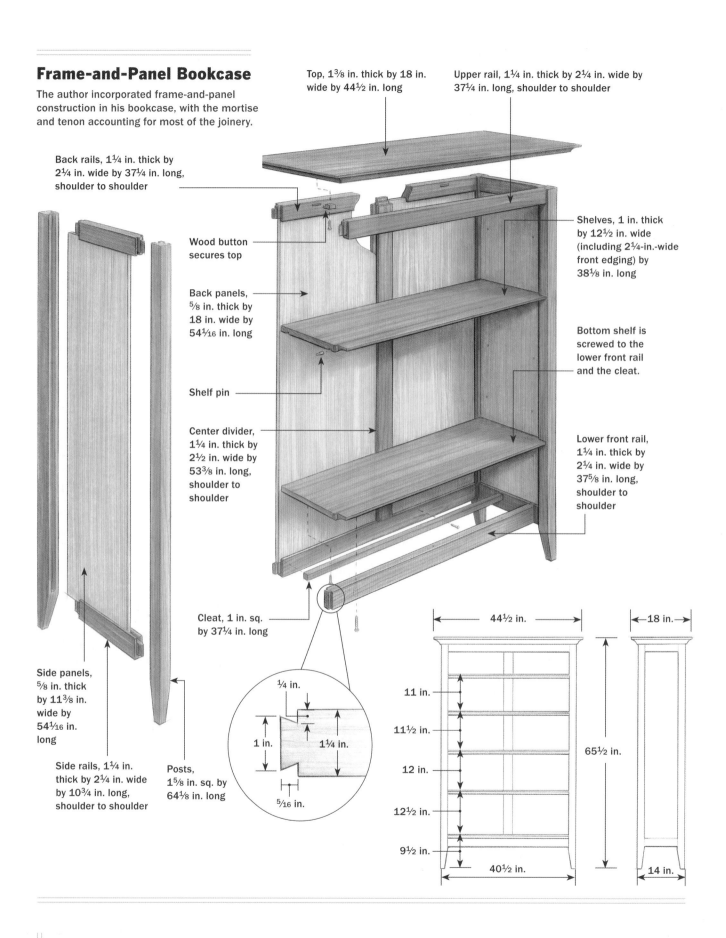

Top, 1³⁄₈ in. thick by 18 in. wide by 44½ in. long

Upper rail, 1¼ in. thick by 2¼ in. wide by 37¼ in. long, shoulder to shoulder

Back rails, 1¼ in. thick by 2¼ in. wide by 37¼ in. long, shoulder to shoulder

Wood button secures top

Back panels, ⁵⁄₈ in. thick by 18 in. wide by 54¹⁄₁₆ in. long

Shelf pin

Center divider, 1¼ in. thick by 2½ in. wide by 53³⁄₈ in. long, shoulder to shoulder

Shelves, 1 in. thick by 12½ in. wide (including 2¼-in.-wide front edging) by 38⅛ in. long

Bottom shelf is screwed to the lower front rail and the cleat.

Lower front rail, 1¼ in. thick by 2¼ in. wide by 37⅝ in. long, shoulder to shoulder

Side panels, ⁵⁄₈ in. thick by 11³⁄₈ in. wide by 54¹⁄₁₆ in. long

Side rails, 1¼ in. thick by 2¼ in. wide by 10¾ in. long, shoulder to shoulder

Posts, 1⅝ in. sq. by 64⅛ in. long

Cleat, 1 in. sq. by 37¼ in. long

¼ in.

1 in.

1¼ in.

⁵⁄₁₆ in.

44½ in.

18 in.

11 in.

11½ in.

12 in.

12½ in.

9½ in.

65½ in.

40½ in.

14 in.

Cut grooves to accept the fir panels.
To cut stopped grooves in the posts, first clamp an extra-long auxiliary fence to the rip fence of the tablesaw, then clamp a stop block to the auxiliary fence. Use a dado head to cut the grooves.

Square the corners. The dado head leaves a rounded portion at the stopped end of the grooves. A chisel makes them square in short order.

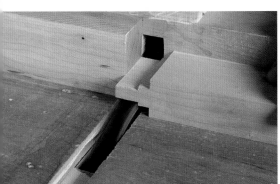

Two-step tenon. Use a dado head to cut the tenons. First clamp a stop block to the fence to establish the tenon length. Then cut the portion of the tenon that fits into the groove. To create the step, reset the blade height and reposition the stop block, as shown.

Cut the Joinery for the Posts and Rails

The rails have stepped tenons that fit snugly in both the panel groove and the mortise, adding strength to the joints.

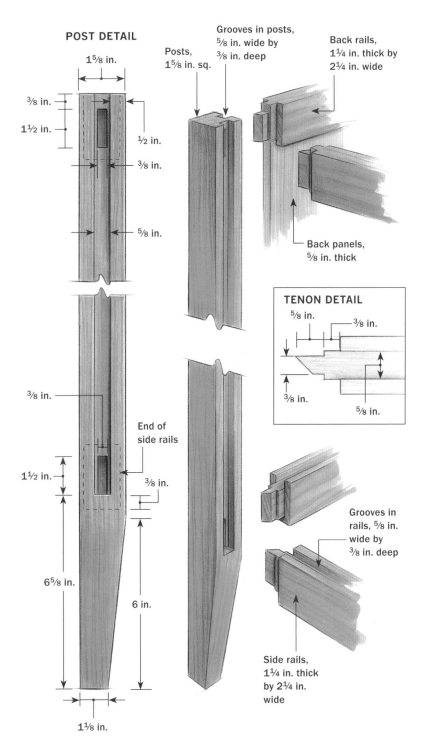

POST DETAIL

1⅝ in.

⅜ in.
1½ in.
½ in.
⅜ in.
⅝ in.

⅜ in.

End of side rails

1½ in.
⅜ in.

6⅝ in.
6 in.

1⅛ in.

Posts, 1⅝ in. sq.

Grooves in posts, ⅝ in. wide by ⅜ in. deep

Back rails, 1¼ in. thick by 2¼ in. wide

Back panels, ⅝ in. thick

TENON DETAIL

⅝ in.
⅜ in.
⅜ in.
⅝ in.

Grooves in rails, ⅝ in. wide by ⅜ in. deep

Side rails, 1¼ in. thick by 2¼ in. wide

sawn Douglas fir. So I used cherry for the frame parts, the top, and the front edging on the shelves. The quartersawn fir is incorporated into the panels.

Sometimes, when wood is moved from one location to another, the new conditions of temperature and humidity can cause it to warp a bit, often within a few hours of the relocation. So once I have all of the oversize stock together in my shop, I like to give it a few weeks to acclimate to its new temporary home. Then, after rough-milling the stock, I allow it to sit for another day before cutting it to final size. Any last-minute twisting or cupping gets removed at this stage.

Construction is straightforward

I began by gluing up blanks for the ⅝-in.-thick side and back panels. To do that, I resawed 8/4 fir, book-matching the panels to add a balanced look.

All of the shelves were made from commercially available 5/4 by 12-in.-wide stair stock. However, the front of each shelf received an edging of 2¼-in.-wide cherry, so the bookcase ends up with an all-cherry look when viewed from the front. The cherry edging has another plus. Because fir sometimes can be splintery, the cherry almost eliminated any splitting out when the coves were cut.

Most of the frame was put together with mortise-and-tenon joints. The one exception is a sliding dovetail joint that I used to connect each end of the lower front rail to the lower side rail.

To accept the panels, I cut ⅝-in.-wide grooves into the posts, the center divider, the side rails, and the upper and lower back rails. The grooves in the posts were stopped about 7 in. short of the bottom. Then, at each stopped end, I used a bench chisel to square up the rounded portion.

After all of the joints had been cut and fitted, I cut the panels to final length and width. All of the panel surfaces were sanded through 220 grit. After that, I applied four coats of tung oil to each panel.

Oil finishes sometimes bleed from the wood pores while drying. When that happens, the finish often ends up with tiny beads of hardened oil, and that can give the finish a slight roughness. So once a coat had dried, I sanded it lightly with 1,000-grit sandpaper wetted with mineral oil. The wet-sanding removed any beads that formed. Then, I wiped the sanded surfaces with a clean, soft cloth and allowed the mineral oil to dry. Once it was dry, I added the next coat of tung oil.

Assembly begins at the back. With all of the parts cut and fitted to his satisfaction, the author is ready to begin assembly. First, though, he applies four coats of tung oil finish to all of the panels.

Assemble the back. The two back panels are slipped into the grooves in the frame parts and then clamped.

Add the remaining frame-and-panel parts. Once the back glue-up has dried, the remaining frame-and-panel parts are added in one big glue-up. First, the lower front rail is assembled to the two lower side rails and then all four of the side rails are added to the back posts. Following in quick succession are the side panels, front posts, and the upper rail (left). An assortment of clamps keeps the joints tight until the glue sets up (above).

Assembly starts with the back section

I started the assembly process by putting together all of the parts that compose the back section—the two back posts, the upper and lower back rails, the center divider, and the two back panels. Except for the panels, all of the mating surfaces were glued together. That way, the panels are free to expand and contract in width as their moisture content changes.

Once the back section was dry, I joined most of the remaining parts in one big glue-up. I began by adding the lower front rail to the two lower side rails. After that, the four side rails were assembled to the mortises in the two back posts. Then I simply slid the side panels into the grooves in the side rails. Once the upper front rail was mounted, I added the clamps and checked the frame for square.

While the clamped parts dried, I cut the top and the shelves to final width and length. Then I cut the coved profile. Although you can use a special shaper cutter, I cut the coves in two steps using a tablesaw and a router table. For this technique, I used a dado head

The lamb's tongue. A small bevel at each corner of the top is cut with a chisel to help soften the hard right angle of the edges.

Remove most of the waste. Make a series of increasingly deeper cuts with the dado head. A test block, with the cove profile marked on the end, helps establish the location of the cuts.

Cut the Coves in Two Steps

Applying a generous cove to the exposed edges of the top and the shelves makes the parts look thinner, giving this large bookcase a lighter feel.

Make a series of cuts using the router table and a large cove bit. Use a curved scraper to smooth out any wavy edges left by the cove bit.

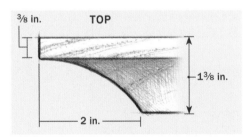

³⁄₈ in.   **TOP**

1³⁄₈ in.

2 in.

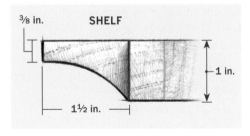

³⁄₈ in.   **SHELF**

1 in.

1½ in.

in the tablesaw and made several passes to remove most of the waste stock. Then, using a ¾-in.-radius cove bit mounted in a router table, I made a series of additional passes. The cove bit easily conforms to the profile, so it's more efficient at removing waste stock than a straight-sided dado head is.

After the work with the cove bit had been completed, I was left with a wavy profile that needed to be smoothed out. A curved scraper came in handy here.

Once all of the coves had been cut and smoothed, I used a chisel to cut a small bevel,

Attach the bottom shelf. The bottom shelf is secured by driving screws up through the cleat and the lower front rail. To allow the shelf to expand and contract with changes in humidity, the author uses a rat-tail file to slot the portion of the hole that accepts the shank of the screw.

Add the top. After cutting several shallow slots in the upper rails, the author slips a notched wood button in each slot. Then the buttons are screwed to the underside of the top.

sometimes called a lamb's tongue, where the coves meet at the corners. Granted, it's a small detail, but it brings the corners to a crisp point. Also, to anyone looking at the bookcase, the bevel sends a subtle message that this isn't a production piece but was made by a craftsman.

At this point in the construction, all five of the shelves were just about complete. I simply had to notch the front and back corners to fit around the inside corners of the four posts.

I used a simple jig to drill the holes for the pins that support the shelf. And here I had two options. I could have drilled a series of holes, spaced evenly apart, to provide adjustability. Or, if the client didn't want to see all of those holes, I could have simply drilled them where the shelves were going to go.

To add strength to the bookcase, the bottom shelf was fixed in place. It rests on two parts: the lower front rail and a cleat that's screwed to the inside face of the lower back

Straightforward construction. You won't need much more than a weekend or two to build this elegant bookcase.

rail. Six screws hold the shelf in place. The screws were driven up through counterbored holes in the lower front rail and the cleat.

Next, I sanded all exposed surfaces until smooth, except for the panels, with 220-grit paper. Then, again excepting the panels, I added four coats of tung oil, sanding between each coat with 1,000-grit paper while the oil was still wet.

To allow the top to expand and contract in width as the humidity changes, I attached it to the frame using eight small wood buttons. A final rubdown with a soft, dust-free cloth completed the project.

A Classic Bookcase

GREGORY PAOLINI

Anyone familiar with American furniture would immediately identify this bookcase as an Arts and Crafts design. However, it differs from traditional pieces in two important ways. Arts and Crafts furniture is usually made from quartersawn white oak, but I built this bookcase from curly cherry. Traditional Arts and Crafts pieces are joined with mortises and tenons, whereas I use a modern variation—the floating tenon.

In floating-tenon joinery, a wooden spline (the floating tenon) joins mortises routed in both pieces. I find floating-tenon joinery to be much faster than traditional mortise-and-tenon and plenty strong.

I spent time choosing highly figured boards for the front rails and the side panels, which will be most visible. The back is of shiplapped cherry, resawn (sliced in half to produce two thinner boards) from 4/4 stock. Shiplapping is a method of slightly overlapping boards by rabbetting the opposite edge of each side. Shiplapped boards rarely end up sitting exactly flush with each other. Those who don't like that look might substitute plywood or tongue-and-groove boards for the back.

Prepare the stock before you begin

As with all projects, I make sure the lumber is dried properly, and acclimate it to my shop for a couple of weeks. After that, I rough-

Bookcase Anatomy

Built from cherry and joined with floating tenons, this case is a modern take on an Arts and Crafts classic. The tenons provide rigidity so the sides and back can float within the rails and stretchers. The side panels are book-matched and the back is shiplapped.

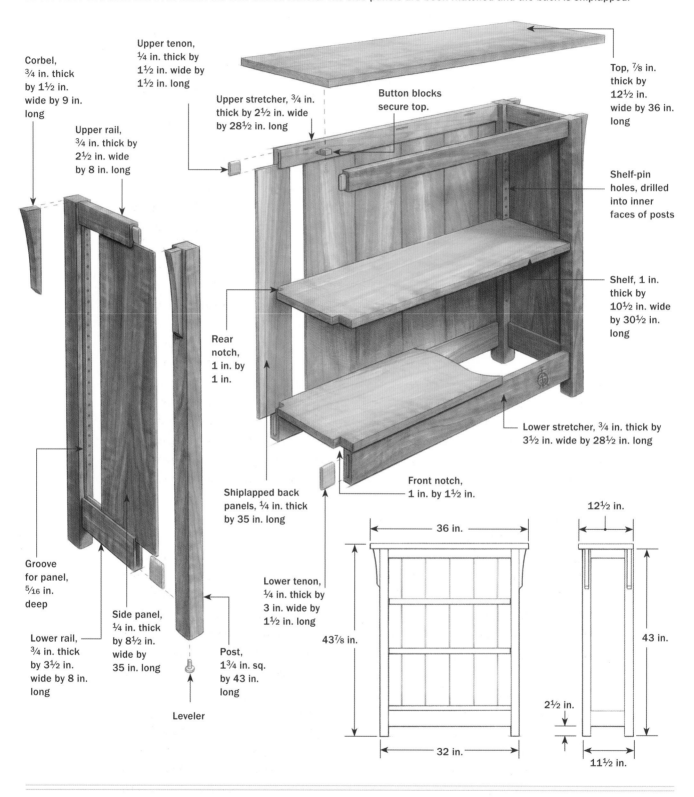

Corbel, ¾ in. thick by 1½ in. wide by 9 in. long

Upper tenon, ¼ in. thick by 1½ in. wide by 1½ in. long

Upper stretcher, ¾ in. thick by 2½ in. wide by 28½ in. long

Button blocks secure top.

Top, ⅞ in. thick by 12½ in. wide by 36 in. long

Upper rail, ¾ in. thick by 2½ in. wide by 8 in. long

Shelf-pin holes, drilled into inner faces of posts

Rear notch, 1 in. by 1 in.

Shelf, 1 in. thick by 10½ in. wide by 30½ in. long

Groove for panel, 5/16 in. deep

Lower rail, ¾ in. thick by 3½ in. wide by 8 in. long

Side panel, ¼ in. thick by 8½ in. wide by 35 in. long

Post, 1¾ in. sq. by 43 in. long

Leveler

Shiplapped back panels, ¼ in. thick by 35 in. long

Lower tenon, ¼ in. thick by 3 in. wide by 1½ in. long

Front notch, 1 in. by 1½ in.

Lower stretcher, ¾ in. thick by 3½ in. wide by 28½ in. long

36 in.

12½ in.

43⅞ in.

43 in.

32 in.

2½ in.

11½ in.

Floating Tenons Join the Case

Cut from scrap, tenons should be thick enough to slip into the mortise with hand pressure and slightly undersize in width to give excess glue somewhere to go during assembly.

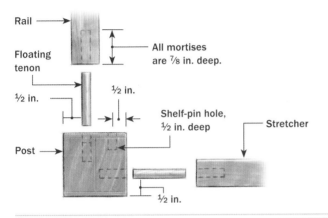

Rail

Floating tenon

½ in.

½ in.

All mortises are ⅞ in. deep.

Shelf-pin hole, ½ in. deep

Post

Stretcher

½ in.

cut all of the boards slightly oversize and let them sit for an extra day or two in case the wood still wants to shift a bit.

Face-jointing is a critical, but often over-looked, step in dressing lumber. Jointing one face flattens the board, removing flaws such as cupping or mild twisting. To keep track of it as a reference surface, I mark the jointed face with chalk. After face-jointing, I square one edge of each board, being sure to feed it through the jointer with the flattened face against the fence. When I plane the stock to thickness, the jointed face rides across the bed of the planer, ensuring a flat board.

Like the shiplapped back, the side panels are resawn from 4/4 stock. I leave the stock destined for resawing as thick as possible, planing it only to remove the rough face.

My bandsaw is a basic 14-in. model with a 6-in. riser block to add capacity. It's not ter-ribly powerful, so to help it out while resaw-ing wide stock, I start by kerfing both edges

of the boards on the tablesaw. This leaves less wood in the center of the board to bandsaw and the kerfs help guide the bandsaw blade to ensure a straighter cut.

The boards resawn for the back are planed to finished thickness and then weighted down in a stack to keep them flat. These boards can vary in width, which adds a little character to the bookcase, and should be left a little oversize for fitting to the back of the case.

The side panels are book-matched (resawn panels are glued edge to edge so that the grain of each mirrors the other). When the glue has cured, scrape away the excess, and plane the sides to their final thickness. As with the back, I leave the side panels oversize and fit them to the case later.

I couldn't find any 8/4 stock for the posts, so I glued each one from two pieces of 4/4 stock planed to ⅞ in. To give the illusion that these posts came from one piece of wood, I ripped some cherry to about ⅛ in. thick, and used it as a thick veneer on the sides of the posts that showed the glue-line. Although this technique also results in gluelines, they're so close to the corners of the posts that they're barely noticeable.

Floating tenons speed construction

As with traditional mortise-and-tenon joints, floating tenons should be about one-third the thickness of the stock. In this case, the finished thickness of the bookcase rails is ¾ in. and the tenons are ¼ in. thick. Accordingly, I cut the mortises with a ¼-in. spiral upcutting bit on a plunge router using a simple jig.

I make the tenons by ripping and planing lengths of stock to fit the mortises. The tenon edges are bullnosed on a router table. The tenons should be thick enough to slip into the mortises with hand pressure and a little

Routing the rail mortises. Fitted with a guide bushing the same diameter as the slot, a plunge router easily mortises the ends of the rails and stretchers.

A SIMPLE MORTISING JIG

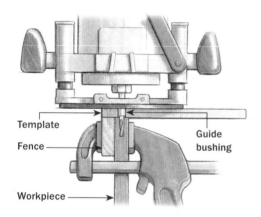

Template

Fence

Guide bushing

Workpiece

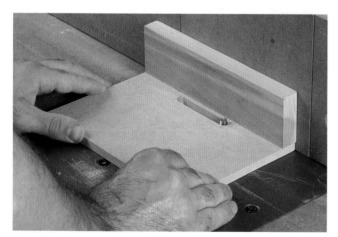

Slot the jig on a router table. The jig's hardwood fence rides along the router table's fence, accurately slotting the jig's medium-density fiberboard (MDF) base.

Mark centerlines on both the jig's slot and the workpiece. Line up the centerlines and clamp the stock in the jig.

Routing the post mortises.
When mortising the posts, there's not much surface area to support the router. A second post laid beside the workpiece adds support.

SUPPORTING THE ROUTER

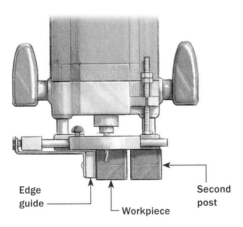

Edge guide

Second post

Workpiece

undersize in width to give air and excess glue somewhere to go. The mortises are just over ¾ in. deep; I cut the tenon stock into 1½-in.-long pieces.

Mortise and groove the frame

I mortise the posts using a plunge router and a fence. The bit is the same ¼-in. spiral upcutting bit used to mortise the rails and stretchers. I have to set up the router and fence anyway to groove the posts for the side panels and shiplapped back, and the panels are the same thickness as the tenons. So, cutting the mortises at the same time is only a matter of deepening the groove at the top and bottom of the post. To provide additional support for the router, I place a second post alongside the one being routed (see "Bookcase Anatomy" on p. 160). So as not to strain the router bit, it's important to make several light passes instead of one heavy pass. When a router bit spinning at 20,000 rpm breaks, bad things happen. Before putting the router away, I cut small grooves in the upper rails and stretchers. Later on, I will use them to secure the top with button blocks (see the drawing).

Bookcases get loaded with hundreds of pounds of books, and it's tough on the joints if the piece is not level. I like to add adjustable levelers to the bottoms of the posts. I use common metal pad levelers available at most hardware stores, and screw them into threaded inserts that I install in the base of each post.

Grooves for the back and side panels.
Mill the grooves in the rails and stretchers on the tablesaw. This method is a safer, easier alternative to routing the thin edges of these pieces.

A plunge router fitted with a fence mills the grooves in the posts. Use the same router setup used to cut the mortises in the posts.

The next operation on the posts is to drill an array of holes for the adjustable shelf pins. To keep them out of view, I locate the bores for these pins on the inner faces of the posts. I use a jig that I made, with holes drilled at the cabinetmaker's standard 32 mm spacing. These holes are drilled to accept a ⅜-in. router bushing. With my plunge router so equipped, I "drill" the holes with a ¼-in. spiral upcutting bit.

Finally, I ease the bottoms of the posts by holding them at an angle and spinning the bottoms against a sander.

Dry-assemble to check final dimensions

With all the joints cut, I dry-assemble the bookcase and measure for the back and side panels. Both the side panels and the back will expand and contract due to seasonal humidity—about ⅛ in. per foot of width.

How you size the panels depends on the season. For example, if it's humid, the panels should fit snugly because they'll dry and shrink when the season changes. If your shop is very dry, keep the fit looser (to allow some expansion).

Now is also the time to measure the final length and depth of the shelves and lay out the notches at the corners where the shelves will fit around the posts. I cut these notches on a bandsaw, but you could just as well use a handsaw or jigsaw. Leave a 1/16-in. space between each post and its corresponding notch to accommodate seasonal movement.

After I have sized the side panels, back, and shelves, I do one last dry-fit and make any required adjustments. When I know everything will fit together, I sand all the pieces to 220 grit.

Making and attaching the corbels is the final step before finishing. I bandsaw them,

Prefinishing saves hours of time cleaning glue squeeze-out. Shop towels shoved into the mortises keep them finish free to ensure glue adhesion (above). Glue-up starts with the sides (right). Allow them to dry overnight before removing the clamps.

then smooth the sawn surfaces with a spokeshave and a little sanding. Because the corbels are only ornamental, they can be attached with brads and glue.

Finished—but not done

To minimize the problems glue squeeze-out can cause, I finish all the parts before assembly. Prefinishing takes discipline; after all this time, you just want to see the bookcase take shape. But finishing the parts first means you won't have to spend tedious hours trying to clean up glue squeeze-out later.

I apply a coat of Zinsser Bulls Eye SealCoat™ sanding sealer over the raw wood to minimize grain raising. The sealer also adds a nice amber hue typical of traditional oil-based finishes, but lacking in the water-based ones I use. I let it dry overnight, then apply several coats of Minwax polycrylic. Be sure to apply the same number of coats to all sides of the pieces to minimize the chance of the wood warping.

Top off the assembly with the final side. Use pine blocks on each side of the corbels to transfer clamping pressure to the posts.

Next come the stretchers and the back. You may want to enlist a helper when putting together the shiplapped back.

Add the top and shelves, and this new heirloom is ready. The shelves are all removable, resting on shelf pins or the bottom stretchers, and notched to fit around the posts.

Putting it all together

I assemble the bookcase in stages, starting with the sides. The best way I've found to glue the mortises and tenons together is to apply a thin bead of glue along the top of the mortise and let gravity pull it down. As soon as I've clamped the assembly, I check it with a carpenter's framing square.

After the sides have cured, I move on to assembling the front and the back. You might want to use polyurethane glue for assembling the back; it has a longer open time than yellow glue.

While clamping the bottom is straightforward, the top with its corbels causes a problem. The solution is to use small pine blocks on each side of the corbels to transmit clamping pressure to the posts. Once the glue has cured, I can easily remove any squeezeout, which doesn't bond to the topcoat very well. Then I attach the top with button blocks to allow for wood movement, and install the shelves. I finish up with a quick coat of wax for its tactile benefit.

Metric Equivalents

INCHES	CENTIMETERS	MILLIMETERS	INCHES	CENTIMETERS	MILLIMETERS
⅛	0.3	3	13	33.0	330
¼	0.6	6	14	35.6	356
⅜	1.0	10	15	38.1	381
½	1.3	13	16	40.6	406
⅝	1.6	16	17	43.2	432
¾	1.9	19	18	45.7	457
⅞	2.2	22	19	48.3	483
1	2.5	25	20	50.8	508
1¼	3.2	32	21	53.3	533
1½	3.8	38	22	55.9	559
1¾	4.4	44	23	58.4	584
2	5.1	51	24	61	610
2½	6.4	64	25	63.5	635
3	7.6	76	26	66.0	660
3½	8.9	89	27	68.6	686
4	10.2	102	28	71.7	717
4½	11.4	114	29	73.7	737
5	12.7	127	30	76.2	762
6	15.2	152	31	78.7	787
7	17.8	178	32	81.3	813
8	20.3	203	33	83.8	838
9	22.9	229	34	86.4	864
10	25.4	254	35	88.9	889
11	27.9	279	36	91.4	914
12	30.5	305			

Contributors

Christian Becksvoort, a *Fine Woodworking* contributing editor, builds furniture in New Gloucester, Maine. He has been doing restoration work at the Sabbathday Lake Shaker community since 1975.

Anatole Burkin, former editor-in-chief of *Fine Woodworking*, is the Group Publisher of *Fine Homebuilding*, *Fine Woodworking*, and *Fine Gardening* at The Taunton Press, Inc.

Steve Casey designs and builds fine custom furniture, cabinetry, and original artwork and has been serving the Los Angeles and Southern California market since 1978.

Charles Durfee builds furniture in Woolwich, Maine.

Garrett Hack, a professional furniture maker, writer, and internationally known teacher, is a *Fine Woodworking* contributing editor.

Steve Latta, a *Fine Woodworking* contributing editor, builds reproduction and contemporary furniture while teaching cabinetmaking at Thaddeus Stevens College of Technology in Lancaster, Pa. He lives in rural Pennsylvania with his wife, Elizabeth, and their three children, Fletcher, Sarah and Grace.

Philip C. Lowe is the master furniture maker and director of The Furniture Institute of Massachusetts (www.furnituremakingclasses. com). Since 1985 he has operated a furniture making and restoration shop in Beverly, Mass.

Martin Milkovits, a furniture maker in Mason, N.H., is a member of the League of NH Craftsmen, Guild of New Hampshire Woodworkers, and the New Hampshire Furniture Masters Association. He has work on permanent exhibit in the Uncle Sam Museum in Sonoma, Calif.

Gregory Paolini owns and operates a custom furniture and cabinetry business near Asheville, NC. He also writes and teaches about woodworking. You can see examples of his work at www.GregoryPaolini.com.

Michael Pekovich, *Fine Woodworking's* executive art director, is also a prolific furniture maker.

Mario Rodriguez is a longtime contributor who teaches at the Philadelphia Furniture Workshop (philadelphiafurnitureworkshop.com).

Matthew Teague lives in Nashville, Tenn., where he builds furniture and writes about woodworking.

Peter Turner is a furniture maker in South Portland, Maine.

Peter Zuerner, owner of Zuerner Design, builds furniture in Middletown, R.I., just a silver-spoon's throw from the historic mansions of Newport.

Credits

All photos are courtesy of *Fine Woodworking* magazine © The Taunton Press, Inc., except as noted below:

Front cover: Main photo by Thomas McKenna. Top to bottom: Anissa Kapsales and Ken St. Onge

Back cover from top to bottom: Steve Scott, Thomas McKenna, and Steve Scott

The articles in this book appeared in the following issues of *Fine Woodworking>*:

pp. 4–13: Shaker Blanket Chest by Charles Durfee, issue 172. Photos by Mark Schofield except for photo p. 5 by Michael Pekovich. Drawings by Fred Carlson.

pp. 14–23: Hickory and Ash Blanket Chest by Peter Turner, issue 203. Photos by Anissa Kapsales. Drawings by Bob La Pointe.

pp. 24–33: Shaker Chest of Drawers by Christian Becksvoort, issue 206. Photos by Anissa Kapsales except for photo p. 24 by Michael Pekovich. Drawings by Bob La Pointe.

pp. 34–41: Classic Shaker Cupboard by Christian Becksvoort, issue 218. Photos by Anissa Kapsales except for photo p. 35 by Dennis Griggs. Drawings by John Hartman.

pp. 42–47: Frame-and-Panel Doors Made Easier by Christian Becksvoort, issue 218. Photos by Anissa Kapsales. Drawings by John Hartman.

pp. 48–57: Shaker Chimney Cupboard by Michael Pekovich, issue 232. Photos by Ken St. Onge except for photo p. 48 by Michael Pekovich and photos pp. 51, 53, 56, and 57 by Rachel Barclay. Drawings by John Hartman.

pp. 58–69: Pennsylvania Spicebox by Steve Latta, issue 196. Photos by Steve Scott. Drawings by Bob La Pointe.

pp. 70–79: The High Art of the Lowboy by Philip C. Lowe, issue 201. Photos by Steve Scott. Drawings by Bob La Pointe.

pp. 80-89: Arts and Crafts on Display by Michael Pekovich, issue 211. Photos by Thomas McKenna. Drawings by Bob La Pointe except for drawings pp. 81 (left), 82, and 83 (except detail drawings) by Dave Richards.

pp. 90-99: The Versatile Huntboard by Garrett Hack, issue 187. Photos by Thomas McKenna. Drawings by Bob La Pointe.

pp. 100–109: Sleek Console Built for Today's TVs by Anatole Burkin, issue 214. Photos by Thomas McKenna except for photo pp. 101 (top left) and 108 (bottom) by Michael Pekovich. Drawings by Bob La Pointe.

pp. 110–124: A Low Console for Home Theater by Steve Casey, issue 200. Photos by Steve Scott except for photos p. 110 and 111 (top right and bottom left) by Dean Della Ventura. Drawings by John Hartman.

pp. 118–125: Wall Cabinet in Cherry by Matthew Teague, issue 180. Photos by Tom Begnal except for photo p. 118 by Kelly J. Dunton. Drawings by John Hartman.

pp. 126–133: A Better Way to Build Wall Cabinets by Garrett Hack, issue 210. Photos by Michael Pekovich. Drawings by Bob La Pointe.

pp. 134–142: Build a Vanity Cabinet by Mario Rodriguez, issue 235. Photos by Thomas McKenna. Drawings by Bob La Pointe.

pp. 143–150: Quick, Sturdy Bookcase by Martin Milkovits, issue 194. Photos by Thomas McKenna. Drawings by John Hartman.

pp. 151–158: Cherry and Fir Bookcase by Peter Zuerner, issue 161. Photos by Tom Begnal except for photo p. 151 by Michael Pekovich, photo p. 155 (bottom) by Kelly J. Dunton, and photo p. 158 by Scott Phillips. Drawings by Bob La Pointe.

pp. 159–166: A Classic Case by Gregory Paolini, issue 179. Photos by Andy Engel except for photos p. 162 by Rodney Diaz. Drawings by Bob La Pointe.

Index

If you like this book, you'll love *Fine Woodworking*.

Read *Fine Woodworking* Magazine:

Get seven issues, including our annual *Tools & Shops* issue, plus FREE iPad digital access. Packed with trusted expertise, every issue helps build your skills as you build beautiful, enduring projects.

Subscribe today at:
FineWoodworking.com/4Sub

Discover our *Fine Woodworking* Online Store:

It's your destination for premium resources from America's best craftsmen: how-to books, DVDs, project plans, special interest publications, and more.

Visit today at:
FineWoodworking.com/4More

Get our FREE *Fine Woodworking* eNewsletter:

Improve your skills, find new project ideas, and enjoy free tips and advice from *Fine Woodworking* editors.

Sign up, it's free:
FineWoodworking.com/4Newsletter

Become a FineWoodworking.com member

Join to enjoy unlimited access to premium content and exclusive benefits, including: 1,400 in-depth articles, over 400 videos from top experts, digital issues, monthly giveaways, contests, special offers, and more.

Discover more information online:
FineWoodworking.com/4Join